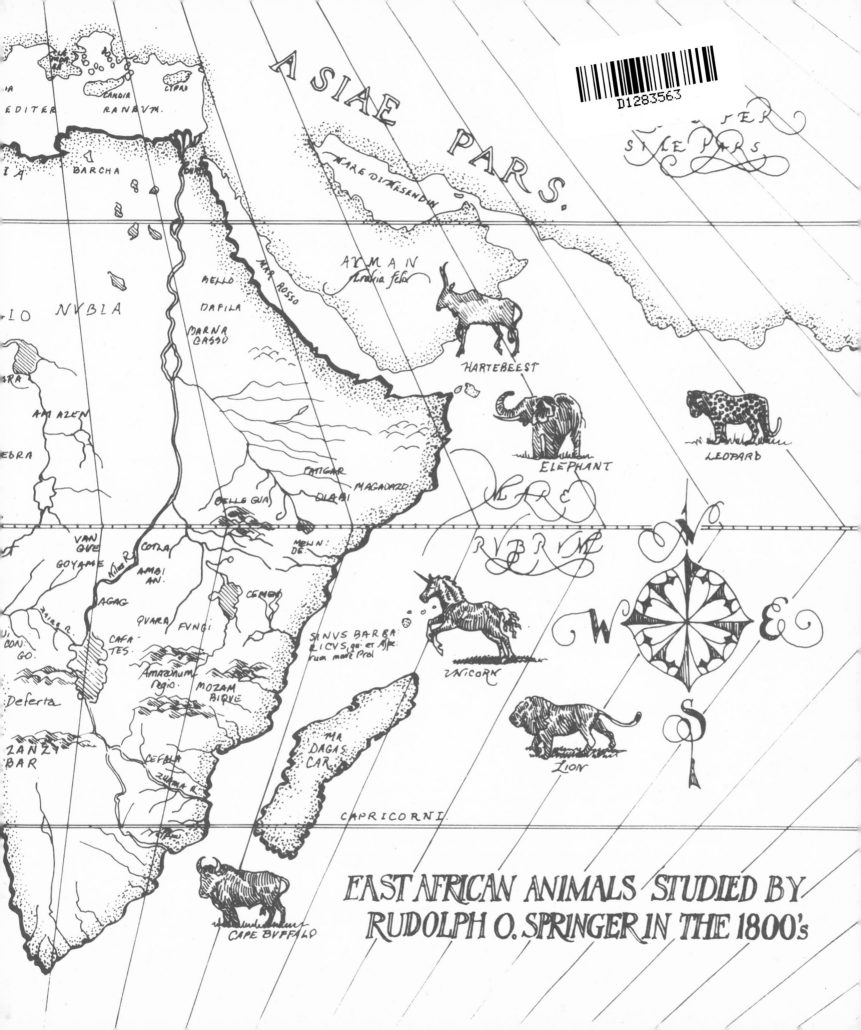

EAST AFRICAN ANIMALS STUDIED BY RUDOLPH O. SPRINGER IN THE 1800's

If man continues to destroy animals and their habitats at the present

rate, then, in the future, creatures as common to us as the

lion and elephant will be as rare and difficult to encounter as is today

the unicorn.

THE UNICORN OF KILIMANJARO

ROBERT VAVRA

Photographs of the author in Africa
by Joseph Saccoman

WILLIAM MORROW AND COMPANY, INC.
New York

For Lorian, mystical muse and enchantress, my friend and friend to all wild creatures—especially to the single-horned, white protagonist of this book.

Library of Congress Cataloging-in-Publication Data

Vavra, Robert.
   The unicorn of Kilimanjaro.

   1. Unicorns.   2. Animals, Mythical—Tanzania—
Kilimanjaro Region.   I. Title.
GR830.U6V376   1988   938.2'454'0967826   88-9270
ISBN 0-688-06850-2

Printed and bound in Spain by Cayfosa, Barcelona.

First Edition

1 2 3 4 5 6 7 8 9 10

Drawings by Lee Mitchelson

Photographic laboratory associate Rick Fabares

Design by the author

Daniel Gómez Casero does not want me to go to Kenya, to leave this ranch in Spain where he is caretaker. How many men or women have the good fortune to know a Kamante, Farah, or Dersu Uzala in their lives? My existence has been enriched by the presence of Daniel . . . In two days I will find if the Africa of childhood dreams still exists and with it—Unicornuus africanus.

July 28, 1987, Tuesday, 7:45 P.M., Cañada Grande, Spain

AFRICA

1987 Elm Tree Unicorn Expedition
July 30–August 31

A Masai child stares. I stand in Karen Blixen's garden, the view from which she describes: "The Mountain of Ngong stretches in a long ridge from North to South, and is crowned with four noble peaks like immovable dark blue waves against the sky."

August 1, Saturday, 9:45 A.M.
Karen Blixen's house, Nairobi

What place more fitting to start this quest for a noble Dark

Continent and a noble, white, one-horned animal? Might Karen

Blixen have sat here in front of her bedroom when she wrote:

"Everything that you saw made for greatness and freedom, and

unequalled nobility"?

August 1, Saturday, 9:45 A.M., Karen Blixen's house, Nairobi

Now adventure begins on foot in golden dawn of African dust. Will Rudolf O.

Springer's East African Elephant, Lion, and Unicorn Field Notes, Including

Formula for Approaching the Above Listed Species at Distances up to Three

Inches Without Danger to the Human Observer *still be valid, though written one*

hundred years ago? Will Ernest Hemingway's inference that a unicorn exists on

Kilimanjaro prove true, though spoken to me almost thirty years ago? I think in

Africa anything is possible.

August 2, Sunday, 5:00 A.M., Foot of Ngong Hills

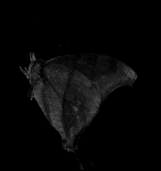

James Michener was right. Cape buffalo are the most

unpredictable, murderous animals in Africa. Even

Springer's formula would not work with them. Still I

love them. The death they represent makes one feel

more vital in their presence. Red-billed oxpecker birds

and club-tailed Charaxes butterflies abundant.

August 2, Sunday, 2:15 P.M., Athi Plains

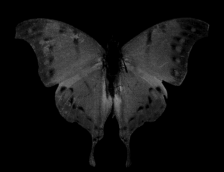

Kilimanjaro is somewhere ahead, protected from

sight by brewing cumulus. Could the view of the

mountain itself be more glorious than the one that

dazzles our eyes? A setting pleading for a unicorn.

August 2, Sunday, 6:15 P.M., Amboseli Gate

. . . awaken sweating from anxious dreams of a vanishing

Africa . . . being witness to an exodus of animals that will

never return. . . . unicorn is swirled in mists of Kilimanjaro,

then disappears—forever. Sounds of dark Africa rescue me

from this nightmare.

August 3, Monday, 4:30 A.M., tent, Amboseli

. . . Masai accompany the sun as it rises from behind

a hill. Not far away, a zebra mare stands with her new

foal. . . . my heart rises with the dawn.

August 3, Monday, 6:05 A.M., Ambosel

. . . feel insignificant in this country of vast landscapes and immense beasts. And more confused than ever by Hemingway's allusion to a unicorn on Kilimanjaro . . . turn my back on the mountain: "Larger than life and white as snow," where could his unicorn be?

August 3, Monday, 9:00 A.M., Ambose

A topi gallops off, accompanied by the thunderheads

that leave Kilimanjaro and the sky clear tonight, but

my mind clouded with the riddle and prospect of

defeat. What, in truth, was Hemingway's leopard

searching for, its eyes blazing like the star-streaked

African sky overhead?

August 3, Monday, 8:15 P.M., Amboseli

. . . new sun illuminates an old tree, perhaps the one

where man was born. . . . field glasses zoom in on

snowcap. See not mountain, only a white shape against

blue. Two white legs! The curve of the white stomach!

The extension of the white neck with head and horn out

of view, to the left, resting on the out-of-sight summit!

The reason for Hemingway's smile! A white snow

unicorn spreads out on the mountaintop.

How could anyone have ever mistaken a rhinoceros for a

unicorn? Rhino . . . disappears into the swirls of gray . . .

recall Peter Matthiessen's experience high near the summit of

Lengai: "Imagine the sight of that dark thing in the smoke of

the volcano; had an African seen it, the rhino might have

become a beast of legend."

August 3, Monday, 5:00 P.M., Amboseli

. . . sudden flash of wings. Putting binoculars to eyes, a topi skull from which the bird has flown, comes into focus. . . . decorated with delicate flowers. So topi and unicorn no longer roam the heights of the Oloololo Escarpment. . . . birds . . . desperate for something to decorate, have made use of the skull. . . . Far below stretches Masai Mara, and the river.

August 12, Wednesday, 1:05 P.M., top of Oloololo Escarpment

As I sit taking notes, think of Odell Shepard's words: "Compared to the unicorn, the hippopotamus is a nightmare, the giraffe highly improbable." Charaxes candiope *butterflies cluster at water's edge.*

August 14, Friday, 2:38 P.M., Loita Hills

Two giraffe appear, turn, and cross in pas de deux. Remember

Karen Blixen's description: "Giraffe, in their . . . inimitable,

vegetative gracefulness . . . rare, long-stemmed, speckled, gigantic

flowers slowly advancing."

August 15, Saturday, 6:30 A.M., edge of Nguruman Escarpment

Bull elephants, like stag unicorns, often engage in mock charges.

Springer was frequently confronted with this seemingly dangerous

situation, in which the observer, if he has been anointed with the

twenty-six-ingredient oil, must merely stand his ground.

August 15, Saturday, 11:15 A.M., edge of Nguruman Escarpment

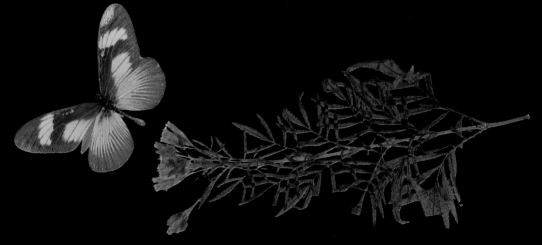

Looking at the elephant, alone in the world . . . while his wonderful

ivory moves from side to side through the grass. I recall, "The shark is

hunted for its fin, the elephant for its tusks, and the rhino for its horn—

then what price the unicorn?"

August 15, Saturday, 3:16 P.M., edge of Nguruman Escarpment

Feel sweat spreading out under arms. Will it wash away oil and will my own smell agitate elephants now towering next to me? Try to keep from making eye contact. Feel air moved by flapping of

. . . topi stamps foreleg nervously and

raises head high. Swing binoculars along

Acacias. Again Karen Blixen's words echo

in my ears: "I had seen the royal lion . . .

in the delicate, spring-like shade of the

broad Acacia trees of his park in Africa."

August 17, Monday, 3:35 P.M.
edge of Nguruman Escarpment

Black-maned lion lifts his head and answers

the distant call of the distant lion. . . . Where

plain curves out of sight, where gray sky

meets gray grass, there is something to

discover that may revolutionize the study of

big cats in the wild.

August 18, Tuesday, 10:45 A.M
edge of Nguruman Escarpment

Lion stops five feet away. Heart pounds. Mind

pounds with Karen Blixen's words: "Lions possess

a greatness, a majesty, which positively instills terror

in the human being and makes one feel later that

everything else is so trivial—thousands of

generations of unrestricted supreme authority, and

one is oneself set back 6,000 generations—suddenly

comes to feel the mighty power of nature, when one

looks it right in the eyes."

Lion suddenly raises his head and stares over right shoulder.

Issues low growl. Cautiously turn to right until lionesses,

grouped closely together, heads held high with curiosity, can

be seen watching us, but do not approach.

August 18, Tuesday, 2:42 P.M., edge of Nguruman Escarpment

Lion . . . circles around me. Try to watch him out of

corner of my eye. "No animal, however fast," wrote

Beryl Markham, "has greater speed than a charging lion

over a distance of a few yards. It is a speed faster than

thought—faster always than escape."

August 18, Tuesday, 3:00 P.M., edge of Nguruman Escarpment

. . . lion gets to his feet . . . His concentration, as he passes,

produces electricity between us. Right now, if just a single wish were

There is mystery in Daniel Ole Mengoru's

dark Masai eyes, flashing and dimming like

zebra in the night. Of one thing only I am

certain, that he has seen the Nentikobe—the

unicorn.

August 20, Thursday, 10:05 A.M., Daniel's manyatta

As try to sleep siesta, Masai Mara

migration stampedes my mind. Tens of

thousands of hoofed, horned animals

Orange, lion tail flowers. . . . stand of yellow fever

trees on left. . . . stepped layers of deep red rocky

mountainside . . . it appears. Nentikobe! Oh,

Daniel was right!

August 20, Thursday, 3:45 P.M., Loita Hills

Could it be that Unicornuus africanus *is so different from other*

races? . . . Tosses head and mane. Rolls eyes. . . . only sounds

now are . . . the sharp smacking of stag's hoofs against red rock.

August 20, Thursday, 3:52 P.M., Loita Hills

Unicorn . . . ending display . . . does half turn,

dashes along ledge of red rock . . . disappears

into vegetation.

August 20, Thursday, 3:52 P.M., Loita Hills

. . . twilight . . . at Daniel's manyatta . . . experience a glow that

persists, within my being and without. . . . is spectacular display of

unicorn, and proof of its existence here, cause for this rare state? I

think not. I think the glow is simply and merely Africa, fitting this

piece of myself into that one empty space in the puzzle of my

existence.

August 20, Thursday, 6:15 P.M., Daniel's manyatta

"An African Native Forest is a mysterious region," wrote Karen Blixen, ". . . the depths of an old tapestry, in places faded and in others darkened with age, but marvellously rich in green shades."

August 21, Friday, 3:20 P.M.
approaching Forest of Lost Children

The falls! First view. White water cascading

between curtains of forest. In that water Daniel

will wash his spear in final Masai ceremony

for approaching Nentikobe.

August 22, Saturday, 11:45 A.M., Forest of Lost Children

73

each falls. . . . Have we arrived at end

world—or is this the beginning?

August 22, Saturday, 12:15 P.M.
Forest of Lost Children

"Nentikobe!" I say . . . wide smile breaks across face

as, unable to contain the joy that surges beneath my

khaki shirt, I glance at Daniel. "Nentikobe!"

August 22, Saturday, 5:25 P.M., foot of Nguruman Escarpment

Suddenly, stag looks away from us and to the left.

Hadada ibis cries from direction of marsh where

unicorn is staring. "Simba!" says Daniel quietly, as a

black-maned lion emerges from the reeds and walks

along edge of water . . .

August 22, Saturday, 5:25 P.M., foot of Nguruman Escarpment

. . . lion glances up, yellow eyes fixed on unicorn. Hadada ibis

calls again. Unicorn then rears high into air . . . strikes with hoofs

. . . then lunges forward running toward . . . lion.

August 22, Saturday, 5:30 P.M., foot of Nguruman Escarpment

Arrive at manyatta. Stop to rest. Masai

celebration. "A Masai warrior is a fine

sight," wrote Karen Blixen. ". . . daring,

Leaning against hut wall. Take notes and rearrange collected pressed flowers and butterflies in field guide. Joy in eyes of Masai children the joy of all children. Here, however, "family," "friend," and "honor" are realities, not empty spoken sounds or meaningless words written on paper.

August 23, Sunday, 1:13 P.M., manyatta, edge of Nguruman Escarpment

. . . far, far off to the right now uncovered by a

drift of cloud is the Mountain of God. Not

Kilimanjaro, as Hemingway wrote, but Ol Doinyo

Lengai. . . . If there is one time and place that I

will stand close enough to a unicorn to feel its

breath, it will be now and here.

August 23, Sunday, 2:23 P.M., edge of Nguruman Escarpment

Conceal myself on overhang that commands

view of forest. . . . Unicorn leaps through

vegetation, leaf patterns of sun and shade

playing like water on silvery back.

August 23, Sunday, 4:28 P.M., edge of Nguruman Escarpment

A lovely young doe whose delicate

beauty belongs in a fairy tale. . . .

stepping through tall reeds, which lash

her silvery sides black with zebra stripes.

August 23, Sunday, 6:08 P.M.
edge of Nguruman Escarpment

. . . sit in midst of decorated, chanting, exotically handsome people around whom spreads the most exotic of landscapes inhabited by the most exotic of creatures.

August 24, Monday, 10:45 A.M., manyatta, Kenya-Tanzania border

Who but a fool would be surprised to find unicorns among these

indigenous beings? Blue salamis *butterfly almost lights on my knee.*

August 24, Monday, 10:45 A.M., manyatta, Kenya-Tanzania border

Running along a dark streambed at edge of the forest, stag

stretches out in full gallop. Masai porter next to me whispers,

"Nentikobe, Nentikobe."

August 24, Monday, 12:15 A.M., Kenya-Tanzania border

Lake is blue or is it pink? Colors merge. Flamingos, like petals from all the

rose gardens of all the world, drift above water or, on slim stems, blossom up

from it.

August 24, Monday, 2:15 P.M. Kenya-Tanzania border

David . . . points to a pennant of green moss into

which have been woven blossoms. Again, the

predominant flower is Notonia abyssinica. *But why*

are birds weaving designs in moss and not in long

hair of unicorns?

August 24, Monday, 5:05 P.M., Kenya-Tanzania border

Stag stands confidently in the magnificence of his maturity. Blue eyes indicate

that he is at least five centuries old. Did Springer see this same animal, then

perhaps dark-eyed, in the early 1880s? Green Charaxes *butterfly flutters*

around horn.

August 24, Monday, 5:22 P.M., Kenya-Tanzania border

. . . in forelock, bluish purple blossoms are scattered as

if by white water of cascade. . . . Solanum incanum?

Clerodendrum myricoides? Pentanisia ourangyne? *. . .*

appear more like Ruellia patula.

August 24, Monday, 5:22 P.M., Kenya-Tanzania border

"Be careful," warns Daniel, "that sound is not good to

him." He glances down at my camera.

August 24, Monday, 5:22 P.M., Kenya-Tanzania border

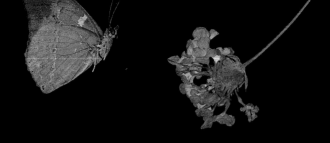

Hearing unicorn warning signal, stag rears slightly, rocks

back, and then, like a white-maned dolphin, plunges . . .

leaving emerald wake strewn with bluish-purple

blossoms.

August 24, Monday, 5:22 P.M., Kenya-Tanzania border

A stag impala . . . turns, and looks at me over shoulder.

. . . Shadows like incoming tide sweep past our tent,

across the clearing and towards wave of green that rises

up against dark sky. Soon all will be black except the

creatures of our imaginations.

August 24, Monday, 6:24 P.M.,
camp between Nguruman Escarpment and Ol Doinyo Lengai

Reach for binoculars. Group

toward us. In focus. Masai. . . .

around their eyes means death

of figures coming

White paint

and rebirth of man.

August 25, Tuesday, 10:45 A.M.,
between Nguruman Escarpment
and Ol Doinyo Lengai

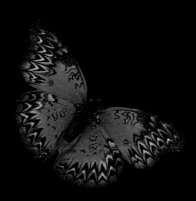

. . . at the back of his head, a half-halo made of sticks

and ostrich feathers. Stands out from group like a black

angel. . . . "The Nentikobe is animal of magic," says the

boy . . . "Would you wish that I take you and your

friend to him?"

. . . then he turns head sharply down toward me,

at the same time voicing a low growl. Pink muzzle

so close that I can feel breath on my hair and face

as I slowly turn eyes away from stag's and gaze

straight ahead as he stares down at me.

August 25, Tuesday, 4:32 P.M.,
between Nguruman Escarpment and Ol Doinyo Lengai

Stag raises muzzle. Trumpets

twice. . . . leaps over log inches

from my face and in an iridescent

flash, disappears into forest,

seemingly guided by direction of

the ibis's flight.

August 25, Tuesday, 4:39 P.M.
Somewhere between Nguruman Escarpment
and Ol Doinyo Lengai

Sit in this house, which before was built of black words on a white

page but now is sound, touch, and color to my mind. . . . here . . .

I wish to finish these journal notes of the 1987 Elm Tree

Unicorn Expedition. Have not left Africa, but already I am

missing it.

August 31, Monday, 1:15 P.M., Karen Blixen's house

As the light moves, I move . . . outside to sit . . . and write at the millstone. A

bushbuck appears . . . at the edge of the garden. Above the trees the four

peaks of the hills "rise like immovable dark blue waves against the sky." . . .

Eyes slide down from mountains onto tree tops and darkening foliage.

Bushbuck is gone. In a little more than seven hours, aboard an Olympic

Airways flight, I will also be gone from here--yet not really gone.

August 31, Monday, 3:30 P.M., Karen Blixen's house

Now I sit in this familiar, Spanish garden . . . A month has passed since I left

Africa. Kilimanjaro, Amboseli, Masai Mara, Athi Plains, Ngong Hills,

Oloololo Escarpment, Loita Hills, Forest of the Lost Children, Nguruman

Escarpment, Natron and Ol Doinyo Lengai: each is a deeply rich tapestry that

hangs, appears and reappears, in the museum of my mind. . . . The tapestries

are changed with the whims of consciousness. Now reality is the smile on my

face. The warm dogs in my arms. The bleached white buffalo skull at my

feet. . . .

September 30, Thursday, 7:30 P.M., Cañada Grande, Spain

Reality is the truth that somewhere high on the Nguruman Escarpment, mane drifting in the wind, horn pointing south toward Ol Doinyo Lengai, the House of God, stands the Nentikobe. Reality is that to him, and to there, I must return.

September 30, Thursday, 7:30 P.M., Cañada Grande, Spain

1987 ELM TREE UNICORN EXPEDITION DIARY

INTRODUCTION

WHEN *Unicorns I Have Known* was published in 1983, I decided that finished were my long and often difficult years of the study and photography of white, single-horned horselike animals. This stand was taken for several reasons. First, I felt that if dozens of creatures in the so-called natural animal world were being brought close to extinction by hunters, poachers, land developers, loggers, and legal and illegal operations that not only eliminate wildlife itself but also its habitat, then to publish further information on the intimate life of unicorns would only place their existence in greater jeopardy. This is taking into account that unicorn sonar and disappearing ability, until now, have afforded almost a magical protection from man. However, with day by day or almost second by second advances in scientific technology, there was and is no guarantee that, somewhere in some laboratory, discoveries aren't being made to undermine these natural unicorn defense measures.

Second, I felt that being a half century old, I should leave further unicorn behavioral studies to younger naturalists. Readers of *Unicorns I Have Known* will remember that much of that book was made possible by a unicorn behavioral study produced prior to my work. This was the field journal of Rudolf O. Springer, which by some strange quirk of luck I had chanced upon in the Madrid Rastro. For persons who have not read my previous study, I quote from it:

My quest for the unicorn began on December 17, 1959, in Surrey at the home of Veronica Tudor-Williams, author of *Basenjis: The Barkless Dogs.* Miss Tudor-Williams, along with the late Dr. James Chapin of the American Museum of Natural History, was one of the first white persons to have studied the Basenji in Africa, where on three occasions she also saw a unicorn roaming the dunes of the Sudan. When she confided her discovery to me this search was instigated, an adventure that fortunately was to take me from England back to Spain, where I found two documents that were invaluable in helping me encounter the world's only large land mammal that—until fifteen years ago—had never been photographed.

In 1960 an American scholar who was doing research at the Archives of the Indies in Sevilla told me of a letter in which Bernal Díaz del Castillo mentioned having observed a unicorn during one of the Cortez expeditions to the New World. Fortunately, I saw and translated that piece of correspondence (which also contained a sketch of a unicorn in the margin) two weeks before—in a folder of priceless papers, including a Christopher Columbus signature—it was stolen from the Archives.

The second document, and the most important to my quest, was a journal that I purchased for 200 pesetas (about 3 U.S. dollars then) in January of 1961, in the Madrid flea market. As far as I know, this ninety-six-page volume is the first serious complete unicorn behavioral study in existence. Dated "1836, Harar" and signed "Rudolf O. Springer," it is in English, using American spelling, and contains detailed drawings and explicit written descriptions of its subject's history, appearance, and habits. Though Veronica Tudor-Williams's account of having seen unicorns in the Sudan and the words of Bernal Díaz del Castillo were convincing, it was the Springer study that confirmed for me the authenticity of an animal that, until then, seemed destined to remain caged up in mythology.

Although my unicorn discoveries were celebrated in magazines such as *Life* and *Bunte,* and in edition after edition of *Unicorns I Have Known,* translated into every language from Spanish to Japanese, I must admit that most of the credit belongs to Rudolf Springer, for not a page could have been written or picture taken had it not been for the unicorn world that his journal opened to me. If I read Springer's journal once, I read it a thousand times. And frequently as I thumbed those well-worn pages, I wondered, but without giving it a great deal of thought, why his unicorn studies in East Africa were limited to a few paragraphs.

As a child naturalist, I loved East Africa only after family and life itself. Kenya's and Tanganyika's wild creatures, people, and geography left my mind in a stampede of unsettling golden dust that would forever cloud my imagination in wonderment. Then why had Springer, who seemed almost a mirror of myself, devoted so little space to this last Eden on earth, the one place, more than any other, where one would expect to find all of the animals we imagine to have boarded the ark, including the unicorn, which supposedly opted to swim? That question remained somewhat of an anxiety to me until nearly two years ago.

The day before Christmas, 1986, the mailman delivered a slim parcel to my brother's house in California, where I was staying. The package had been originally sent to my publisher, William Morrow, in New York, who in turn had mailed it to my town address in Sevilla, Spain. There, a friend had forwarded it to me in El Cajon together with some mundane correspondence.

The brown parcel contained a very short note, which read:

Dear Mr. Vavra: Some years ago I was given your book, *Unicorns I have Known*, for Christmas and you can imagine my astonishment when I came across "Rudolf O. Springer," which is the name of a bachelor great-great-uncle of mine who had infrequently been mentioned by my grandmother as "that red-haired, ne'er-do-well, screwball explorer." After reading your book, I remembered that we had an old steamer trunk in the garage, things my grandmother had in her attic and which were brought over here when she died. Your book made me curious, so I decided, one rainy afternoon when my children were off skiing and my husband was out of town, to open that trunk and see if I could find any kind of reference to this long-deceased relative or whether he was even the same person that you mention in your study.

I must have spent an hour going through the contents of that trunk, mostly faded photographs, some of which were identified as to who the person was on the back side. There were other letters, some army medals and photographs and a diary of my mother's brother who was killed in France during the First World War.

It was when I was returning all of these things to the trunk, disappointed at not having found anything mentioning Rudolf O. Springer, that I noticed a bulge in one of the pasted-on cloth pockets at the back of the trunk. Tired and slightly bored at looking through all of the old photographs, most of the people in which I didn't know, I almost piled those things back in without looking at the contents of the cloth pocket. But I did pull a brown envelope out from it that was so dry and old it almost fell to pieces in my hands. Carefully, I removed the contents out of it, and you can imagine my tremendous surprise when I found the sixty-four pages that I include here.

Mr. Vavra—I put this material in your hands because I also love unicorns. I realize that I could probably make a lot of money by selling these secrets to some commercial wild animal dealers or hunters. But like you, I hope that unicorns will always run free. I would appreciate it if you keep me anonymous if you ever publish anything about my great-great-uncle's discoveries in East Africa. God Bless you.

Signed ____.

The document, which had been sent to me from Corsicana, Texas, included sixty-four hand-written pages that appeared to have been destined for a bound book, perhaps for the Springer unicorn behavioral study that has been in my possession for thirty years. In this new material there was one page that bore the title printed in block capital letters *EAST AFRICAN ELEPHANT, LION, AND UNICORN FIELD NOTES, INCLUDING FORMULA FOR APPROACHING THE ABOVE LISTED SPECIES AT DISTANCES UP TO THREE INCHES WITHOUT DANGER TO THE HUMAN OBSERVER.* Beyond question, the handwriting was Springer's. The page upon which it was written was identical to that of the journal. In fact, a stain, which I would assume to be water, since Springer was a teetotaler, marred the bottom edges of the journal in my possession. It also blemished the sixty-four pages sent to me by this woman who was sure to be the great-great-niece of the man who had made possible my unicorn findings.

As I read that familiar script on those sixty-four magical pages, things fell into place that until then had been mysteries. How, I had always wondered, had Rudolf O. Springer been able to approach unicorns at distances so close, when I could only fantasize about being in such near proximity to the animals I studied? And if there had been a method for doing so, why had he not described it? I sometimes chalked his close encounters up to good luck and more often to the fact that he lived over one hundred years ago when the creatures of this earth were not as harassed and menaced by man as they are today.

In his East African observations, Springer was as detailed and complete as he had been in his other study. It was intriguing to think that this frail, red-headed, dedicated American had been doing close-range studies of African mammals over a hundred years before George B. Schaller, Jane Goodall, Ian Douglas-Hamilton, Dian Fossey, and Mark and Delia Owens would even arrive on the scene to do their own incredible and invaluable fieldwork.

On page six of these notes, Rudolf Springer describes in detail a formula that allows the behavioralist to actually approach and observe unicorns in such a way that the animal takes only slight notice of the human, later paying little or no attention at all to him or her. Precise instructions were listed for vocally summoning the animals to the observer, with tone, rhythm, and pitch of call described minutely, to the extent of actually providing musical notes as aids for the reader. But equally fascinating—and this made my heart pound—was the fact that Springer said that his formula had been effective with elephants, lions, and most of East Africa's other big game, with the exception of the Cape buffalo.

Suddenly, my mind was overloaded with excitement. If the words on these pages were true, I would be able to observe and photograph unicorn rites and rituals that in my previous study had taken place too far from the camera to be discernible. In *Unicorns I Have Known* these rituals had to be illustrated from my verbal descriptions, by Barbara Chance in supplementary drawings. But even more exciting, this formula also applied to other African mammals, not only to herbivores, but also to carnivores. Suddenly, I could envision myself, like Mowgli and his animal friends, roaming the African plain with an immense, maned lion or sitting on a stump surrounded by elephants, their ears fanning me as their trunks cooled the air.

The Approach Formula, as it may be simply called, was described in a four-phase plan. Obviously, although many of the persons who read this book have the best intentions, it is also true that the book will fall into the hands of other people who cannot be trusted. For this reason it is impossible to share Springer's formula here. It is enough to say that of the four steps, one deals with the olfactory sense, one with sound, and two with completely secret materials and methods. Of the four, the process that deals with the olfactory sense seemed the most difficult to achieve. The other three depended more or less on the observer alone, and few outside materials. The olfactory phase, however, required the creation of a body oil, the ingredients of which appeared at first complicated and difficult to obtain. Of the twenty-six materials and liquids necessary for the creation of this oil, I was within a short time able to accumulate twenty-one. Here, I must express my deepest gratitude to friends and animal people Rich Massena and Alan Roocroft of the San Diego Wild Animal Park, who, although in the beginning may have found my requests seemingly "off-the-wall," are good enough friends to have supplied me with the needed items even though the materials were frequently disagreeable (actually disgusting to most people) and dangerous to obtain.

Finally, of the twenty-six properties needed for the oil formula, all were in my possession with the exception of two, which seemed almost impossible to acquire. It was then that I met Lorain Stadler, a Rima-like girl, and she, being herbologist, mystic, unicorn and animal lover in general, was able through considerable effort to supply me with the remaining two properties that would make Rudolf Springer's Approach Formula complete.

Having this formula in hand, however, still left many questions and doubts swirling inside my head. Rudolf O. Springer's *East African Elephant, Lion, and Unicorn Field Notes, Including Formula for Approaching the Above Listed Species at Distances up to Three Inches Without Danger to the Human Observer* had been written one hundred years ago. In that time, dozens of species of birds and animals have vanished from this earth—extinct except for their names in zoology books. Did unicorns still exist in Kenya and Tanganyika (now Tanzania)? Springer had safaried there long before Osa and Martin Johnson, Carl Akeley, Karen Blixen, and Ernest Hemingway had been born.

Even if *Unicornuus africanus* were still to be found in the places I was going, would a body oil invented a century ago still be effective with them? If it weren't, my observation and photography would be limited by the distances that inhibited me in *Unicorns I Have Known.* However, if I did encounter *Unicornuus africanus* and the body oil was ineffective, my life and that of my companions would not have been placed in danger, for there is not one recorded account of an unprovoked unicorn attack in the wild. But Springer had underlined the passages giving instructions for use of the oil so deeply that the pen had left an impression on the paper. The formula had always worked—if one used it correctly. Springer had clearly specified that before the body formula is tested with unicorns, it must first be used, and in this order, in confrontations with African elephants, the largest of all land mammals, and with the African lion. He emphasized that if the observer, once in East Africa, did not follow these instructions step by step of first, elephant, second, lion, and third, unicorn, then sighting of East African unicorns would be difficult, and close encounters impossible.

The more I reread the journal, the more intriguing I found its pages. Springer's East African unicorn observations clearly showed that animals found there were extremely different, not in appearance, but in behavior, from those that I had scrutinized in other parts of the world. He described them as being more aggressive and demonstrative in their display rituals. This I found exciting since never had I been able to photograph a stag caught up in any of a number of rituals in which unicorns engage. Although several examples of East African birds weaving flowers in the manes of animals studied were mentioned, it seemed that this symbiotic activity, so characteristic of the avian-mammal relationship that I had encountered in other parts of the world, was not all that common in Kenya and Tanzania. However, he did emphasize that the Hadada ibis was one bird that lived in close association with unicorns and that its presence generally indicated proximity of the animal.

However, while the unicorn's association with other animals, especially lions, was mentioned, it seemed that unicorns would have absolutely nothing to do with African equines—Springer never observed them with zebra or with wild asses. One subject that mystified him was the relationship of unicorns to Cape buffalo, which unicorns seemed to despise. Here, Springer describes an instance in which a stag unicorn was seen to charge, attack, and drive a very large Cape buffalo bull from a section of forest in the Loita Hills. He also emphasized that the Approach Formula was ineffective with *Syncerus caffer* (Cape buffalo), and that it would be suicidal to attempt such an encounter.

This information I found slightly distressing, since the Cape buffalo, along with the lion, is my favorite African animal. Ugly to most persons, killer of more white hunters than any of the other members of the so-called African big-five (elephant, lion, leopard, rhino are the other four), it is a terror to Africans living in the wild. Perhaps it is the sinister, dark appearance of this animal—the exact opposite of the unicorn—and its unpredictability that, oddly enough, I found attractive. Undoubtedly, some of these feelings toward the Cape buffalo could be traced to conversations with Ernest Hemingway and James Michener, who years ago had implanted in me their own feeling of respect and awe for these animals.

In his notes on distribution of unicorns in East Africa, Springer emphasized two locations: the Oloololo Escarpment and the Loita Hills forests southeast to the Nguruman Escarpment (though stray or single animals were now and then reported in other areas). As I read these words, I was puzzled that Mount Kilimanjaro had not been mentioned.

How clearly I remember that evening in 1959 when Ernest Hemingway and I saw on rickety chairs at a lopsided table, its legs sinking unevenly into the sand that skirts Malaga Bay. We talked into the early hours of the morning, when the restaurant was closed and it was almost time for the fishermen to push their boats into the stillness of the Mediterranean. We spoke of Cape buffalo, a mutual favorite; and of antelope and the strange twists and shapes of their horns and ways to recognize them; wildebeests, sitatunga, kudu, impala, sable, roan, hartebeest, gerenuk, topi, Grant's and Thomson's gazelles, eland, waterbuck, oryx, bushbuck, nyala, springbok, and dik-dik. It was then that I asked him hesitantly, "Did you ever hear of a unicorn in East Africa?"

Hemingway's soft eyes twinkled, and his lips, framed by the whiteness of his beard, turned up in smile at the edges, as he softly replied, "You mean an eland with one horn or an oryx seen in profile? Either one could be mistaken for a unicorn, you know."

"No," I persisted haltingly, "I mean . . . I mean a real unicorn."

Hemingway then leaned forward across the table, close enough so that I could see the glistening wine stains that reddened the edges of his mustache and beard. "What do you think the leopard was looking for on Kilimanjaro?" he whispered. "I can guarantee that if you approach Mount Kilimanjaro from the Amboseli side—and you don't even have to climb the mountain—you'll see a unicorn—white as fresh snow—larger than life and . . ."

133

With Ernest Hemingway, 1959

"Papa, it really is awfully late," Mary Hemingway interrupted as she approached her husband and put her hands on his shoulders. "Come now, we must be going. You and Robert can talk tomorrow."

In the days that followed that magical encounter, there were always other people around when I was with Hemingway, which naturally inhibited asking what might to him be embarrassing questions about animals that most humans feel to be creatures of fancy. However, as soon as I returned to Sevilla, I went straight to my bedroom and pulled from a shelf an orange, faded, and fingered Jonathan Cape paperback edition of *The Essential Hemingway*, turned to page 443, and read: "Kilimanjaro is a snow-covered mountain 19,710 feet high, and is said to be the highest mountain in Africa. Its western summit is called by the Masai 'Ngaje Ngai,' the House of God. Close to the western summit there is the dried and frozen carcass of a leopard. No one has explained what the leopard was seeking at that altitude."

Why, then, I wondered, if Hemingway had found a unicorn on Kilimanjaro forty some years ago, had not Springer had similar good fortune in

the even more virgin Africa sixty years prior to that?

In Springer's notes on unicorn sightings he included four pages on locations in Tanzania, all three of which were volcanic craters: Olmoti, and Embagai and Ol Doinyo Lengai. Repeated sightings were made in the craters of Olmoti and Embagai as well as on the slope of Ol Doinyo Lengai and the red-earthed areas northwest of that mountain right up to the Nguruman Escarpment. Several animals were also recorded on the western shore of Lake Natron.

Kilimanjaro, the Loita Hills, the Nguruman Escarpment, Olmoti, Lake Natron, Embagai, and Ol Doinyo Lengai—those names brought back the romance of all my childhood dreams and the books I read after school while my brother and friends were out on the football field. Certain anxiety, however, started to seep into my heart. Springer's study was done a hundred years ago. Hemingway's report was vague and accompanied by a smile. But if I found this worrisome—that unicorns might no longer exist in East Africa—more troubling was the fear that perhaps the East Africa of Hemingway, the Johnsons, Akeley, and Blixen was also as

134

extinct as the single-horned animal protagonist of my quest. Might it not be better to stay home in Spain, to travel to Africa only by way of imagination, and keep alive forever the romance that has existed in me beyond memory?

I met Dr. William Felix Wheeler, an M.D. and photographer, at a book signing in San Diego. That evening, he introduced himself and spoke to me of Africa, where in the last eight years he had traveled over thirty thousand miles in a Land Rover called the Elm Tree, which he maintained in Kenya. Elm Tree had been purchased in London and driven by Dr. Wheeler across the Sahara and the rain forests of Zaire to Nairobi, a long journey. Immediately, my fancy was captured by this man whose pale blue eyes were often fixed in an intense stare that was only occasionally broken as he cleared his throat to suddenly look off in another direction. Whenever he talked of Africa his countenance changed, and it appeared that his experiences there were different from those of any other human being whom I met. From the time of that initial meeting, the same intensity was expressed year after year, when I returned to America, as Bill Wheeler attempted to convince me to accompany him on a trip to East Africa.

It was not until I received the Springer journal that I decided to accept Dr. Wheeler's offer, his experience, company, and Land Rover on a month-long safari to Kenya and Tanzania in search not only of the last large East African animal to be photographed, but of the Africa of my childhood fantasies. Though Wheeler expressed considerable cynicism regarding the existence of unicorns, he did give the assurance that he could introduce me to a country that would be anything and everything except disappointing.

During one of the planning sessions for the Elm Tree Unicorn Expedition (the Elm Tree Land Rover was named for a tree in South Carolina where as a boy Bill Wheeler had played at Tarzan), I was accompanied by Joe Saccoman, a San Diegan in his early thirties. Joe had worked with me as an assistant on several books, including *Unicorns I Have Known*. Suddenly caught up in the excitement of the Elm Tree Expedition, Joe asked if he could come along and said that he would borrow the money in order to do so. It was an attractive opportunity to be able to travel with someone of Bill's experience, enjoying the freedom to stop and go in any direction we wished.

Our initial plan was: On July 12, Bill and Joe would fly from San Diego via Los Angeles, Amsterdam, and Athens for Nairobi. That same day I would leave Sevilla, with connecting flights in Madrid and Athens, to join them later. My concern was that Springer, in his journal, had specifically stated—not once but five times—that the observer must first pass ten days on African soil before anointing his or her entire body with the twenty-six ingredient oil. After that, close encounters could be sought with elephant, lion, and unicorn (again enumerated in that order). He emphasized that if close contact with any three of these mammals was attempted before the tenth day on African ground, the formula for Close Approach would be utterly ineffective and that serious injury or death would surely result from any such attempts. Strange as these instructions seemed, in the past everything that Springer had written had proved true, and only when I had not followed his instructions while gathering material for *Unicorns I Have Known*, had I failed.

It was then decided that upon meeting in Nairobi, we would collect Elm Tree and immediately set out for Tanzania. Once there we would be joined by a Tanzanian antipoaching ranger who would accompany us to the volcanic craters of Olmoti and Embagai, which are so remote that few white persons have ventured there. We would spend three weeks exploring these areas. And we would take a quick look at Ngorongoro Crater and the Serengeti, though I felt the possibility of unicorns living there was at the best remote, as these areas were so overrun with tourists and with scientists doing behavioral studies. From Tanzania we would cross back into Kenya, having then been in East Africa for four more than the ten days required by Springer to put the Approach Formula for elephant, lion, and unicorn observation into action. If unicorns had been found in the two Tanzanian craters, it was agreed that we could always return there from Kenya for further observation and photography guided by Springer's instructions, which would bring us as close as three inches from our wild animal subjects. Total time in Africa would be six weeks, that is from July 13 until August 31.

One of the most intriguing passages in Springer's East Africa journal concerned the relationship of people to unicorns, in this case the Masai. Extensive travels while studying unicorns in a gamut of countries had shown me that the animals seldom had contact with humans. More often than not, animals indigenous to a place were hunted and killed by humans indigenous to the same area. Springer's journal devoted several paragraphs to the relationship of Masai and *Unicornuus africanus*. He writes:

As far as my studies have carried me, never have I encountered a place where man and beast live in harmony such as is found in these lands. The Masai are a noble but warlike people who are often aggressive and hostile in their association with men other than those of their own clan. However, they live in complete peace with the wild animals around them. They seldom hunt and kill for food and then only buffalo and eland—herbivores reminiscent of their own cattle. Other creatures are occasionally slain for ceremonial decorations or clothing. With some frequency, however, they confront and spear to death full-maned lions in shows of bravado. I found it difficult to believe that such noble *Homo sapiens* existed until I actually saw them guiding their herds of cattle through herds of antelope and zebra, the wild beasts showing not the least bit of fear toward the Masai.

After reading this description, one of my prime reasons for making this trip was to see if there really was a place on earth where such pristine coexistence between animal and man still existed.

On April 1, 1987, I returned to Cañada Grande, my ranch in Spain, to finish work on a current book, *Equus Reined*, and prepare it for the printer. Press date was June 20, and estimated printing time was one week. This meant that I would have plenty of time to prepare for the Elm Tree Unicorn Expedition and to meet Bill and Joe in Nairobi on July 14. However, books in their final stages of production are, more often than not, harassed by delays, and such was the case with *Equus Reined*. By the time all of the text had arrived from New York and the color separations were completed in Barcelona, July 1 had passed, and a revised press date was scheduled for the tenth of that same month. Disappointed, I phoned Bill in San Diego and told him that we would not be able to meet as planned, nor would I be able to accompany them to Tanzania for the first leg of the expedition. We would join up on July 20 in Nairobi. They would have to scout Olmoti and Embagai for signs of unicorns without me. Since Joe had accompanied me on previous expeditions, I felt that he had sufficient knowledge to detect evidence of unicorns in the area even if actual sightings were not made.

In the meantime, I read and reread Springer's journal until I practically knew it by heart. I did not reveal the Approach Formula to either Bill or Joe, nor did the thought enter my mind. Not being in possession of the twenty-six-ingredient solution would render any efforts to get closer than the normal flight distance to elephant and lion impossible. Trying it would also place their lives in jeopardy. Anyhow, by the time we were to meet in Nairobi on July 30, they would have been in Africa barely over ten days. This also meant that if I were to arrive on that day, according to Springer's instructions, I could not put his Approach Formula into practice until July 10.

In the tradition of the Springer papers, I decided to keep my own journal in diary form with brief comments about the animals and their habits, along with my immediate impressions. To the layman, this simple, excerpted record of the 1987 Elm Tree Unicorn Expedition may provide an uneventful and dull read, but true unicorn lovers will hopefully find it as intriguing as the experience we lived during those glorious days of last summer in search of Nentikobe.

1987 ELM TREE UNICORN EXPEDITION DIARY

July 26, Sunday, 10:20 A.M., Spain, Cañada Grande

For the past week I have been anxious. Starting a book is often hard on the nerves—I wake up with it in my stomach. But then this diary needs no more searching for a beginning than did Rudolf Springer's East African journal. Thoughts of the moment suffice. It calls for no more story line than the events that will take place between now and midnight, August 31, when I board the Air Olympic flight that will carry me from Nairobi to Athens, Madrid, and finally Sevilla, which is forty-five minutes from this ranch, Cañada Grande.

Here I now sit on the front porch, with the pages of Springer's East African journal. Across the paths of golden sand stretch expanses of lawn to blue legions of lilies of the Nile that surround the garden. Behind the agapanthus are thousands of cannas, which flame red, orange, and yellow; and beyond them altheas stand out mauve against a backdrop of dark, feathery mimosa. Over trees, reflected in the swimming pool, looms a hill that is home to peacocks, Egyptian geese, guinea hens, and California quail.

It is not easy to leave this jungle-colored oasis, surrounded by one hundred and fifty acres of summer-burnt ocher oak groves. Could even Karen Blixen's garden, where I will be in three days, be lovelier?

Several days ago Deedie Wrigley was here with her family from Scottsdale, Arizona, rare visitors to Cañada Grande, where the only open invitation is the one extended to animals and birds. Besides my own footprints, the earth here is seldom marked by human steps except for those of a gnomelike caretaker, called Daniel Gomez Caseró, a sort of Spanish Dersu Uzala or Kamante or Farah. Like them, Daniel is a man of nature, only his language is different.

As I sat on this same porch, Deedie walked across the grass to a three-hundred-year-old oak tree, its far-reaching branches draped with flows of lime-green Boston ivy, a scene that might have been a Rousseau come to life until a dozen white pigeons glided through the foliage to conjure up Disney moments from *Fantasia* or *Bambi*. "Robert," said Deedie, as she looked across the lawn and through the oak trees, "Robert, I just expect a unicorn to appear at any moment."

So if a unicorn could step out of my garden, then the thought of finding one in the last wildlife Eden on earth, East Africa, especially with Rudolf Springer's journal in my possession, seems not at all unnatural. Not the book alone, however, or the anticipation of expected unicorn discovery, *but Africa*, I realized, as I lay in bed this morning, is responsible for the anxiousness that does strange things to my insides. Does the Dark Continent of my childhood imagination, fed by books I read, still exist? Or has it been disfigured beyond recognition, transformed into an immense Lion Country Safari Park filled with placid animals, contaminated by a sideshow of tourists, and sterilized by scientists doing behavioral studies of species that may today roam totally free only in the minds of romantics?

The Dark Continent of childhood I can see as clearly now as I did forty years ago in the enclosures of the Griffith Park Zoo, in Gargantua's cage at the Ringling Brothers and Barnum & Bailey Menagerie, in the dioramas of the L.A. County Museum, or in the Alex Theatre in Glendale. Africa's sounds came from the movie screen, her fragrance from the animals of circuses and zoos, and her images from the few black people I met as a child.

Now as I sit, I wonder at my naiveté. How could anyone expect the Africa of today to vaguely resemble the paradise of yesterday any more than the words *Congo* and *Tanganyika* bear similarity to *Zaire* and *Tanzania*? More remote was the East Africa of Springer's journal written a century ago. A mere twenty years have passed since Peter Matthiessen wrote in *The Tree Where Man Was Born*: "I traveled through Africa . . . and saw the great animal herds of the Serengeti Plains, all of which in 1961 seemed on the point of disappearance." However, Matthiessen found not only the East Africa of his dreams, but describes an animal that he identifies as a beisa oryx, commenting, "The horn was long and straight and whorled; here was the unicorn." In truth, I wondered, had Peter Matthiessen actually encountered a unicorn on the slopes of that mystical and holy volcano? And like many persons of pure heart attempted to confuse hunters and commercial animal dealers by labeling it "oryx"? The place of this encounter was not far from Ol Doinyo Lengai, the volcanic crater that Springer, in his journal, identifies as where repeated unicorn sightings were made.

July 27, Monday, 10:00 P.M., Cañada Grande

Looking out into the darkness, I sit on the porch. Owls cry in the oak groves, crickets sing, colored doves croon mournfully, and somewhere far away, but close enough to be heard, a fighting bull, black and mysterious in the night, lifts his head to roar at the moon, which now shows as crescent, slim, curved, and sharp as his horns. I wonder about Bill Wheeler and Joe Saccoman, already in Africa, having left San Diego on July 12 for Amsterdam, Athens, Nairobi, and Arusha.

What are they doing at this moment, hearing sounds under the same crescent moon that roams all night skies this July 27? Only an hour's time difference separates us. What jungle voices echo around their campfire high on the rim of Embagai crater, or Olmoti crater, or somewhere on the green forested or grassy floors of one of those remote and long-dead volcanoes? Have they found signs of, seen, or photographed unicorns there?

11:30 P.M. Can't get Bill and Joe out of my thoughts, nor the fear that by having stayed in Spain, I may have missed the most significant part of The Elm Tree Unicorn Expedition. Many persons go to Africa, but few visit areas as remote and wild as the places my friends are now exploring. Peter Matthiessen, who had also been fascinated by the area, wrote several passages that, apart from Springer's sightings, convinced me that white, horselike animals with single horns on their heads might be found in Tanzania:

Later, in the Crater Highlands, with a Maasai friend named Martin Mengoriki, I camped on the rim of Embagai, in the hope of going down into its crater. The rim was an alpine meadow dense with flowers, like a circlet around the cloud in the volcano, and under the cloud a crater lake lay in deep forest. All day we waited for a clearing wind, to locate a way down the steep sides, but instead the cloud overflowed onto the meadow, smothering the senses. . . .

In the late afternoon, the meadows cleared. Not far off, a band of ravens connived in a dead

haegenia, the lone, uncommon tree left at this altitude. Before the mists reclaimed it, I climbed the tree and with a panga chopped down dry limbs for a fire. Already, at twilight, it was very cold, but in this hour of changing weathers, odd solitary light shafts, fitful gusts, the mists were lifting, and treetops of the crater sides loomed through the cloud, then the crater floor, and finally the lake, two thousand feet below, where a herd of buffalo stood like dark outcrops on the shore. . . . Then the mists closed, and around the rim of Embagai the fire tones of aloes and red gladioli burned coldly in the cloud. . . .

By morning, clouds had settled heavily into the crater, making the descent impossible. We returned south fifty miles to Ngorongoro.

After years of studying unicorns, if I had ever read a description of a place they were almost certain to inhabit, it was Peter Matthiessen's of Embagai from the crater rim.

July 28, Tuesday, 7:45 P.M., Cañada Grande

I sit on a stone wall, almost five feet high, that circles a twenty-two-acre pasture where goats graze and Spanish mountain pigs root. "How anyone could have ever mistaken a goat for a unicorn or vice versa," wrote Rudolf O. Springer in his field notes, "is beyond even my wildest imagination." The animals are property of Daniel, my caretaker, who like Karen Blixen's devoted Kamante, was a child goatherd. That was in a rural Spain of sixty years ago where poverty was abject, and peasant boys did not go to school.

On the infrequent afternoons when Daniel feels like talking—usually he brushes me off with "Time is gold and one has to know how to take advantage of it"—he often speaks of his childhood. Sometimes he might recite one of the dozens of poems that he has composed about Cañada Grande, all of which are written in his head or heart—none appears on paper unless I have jotted it down.

Sometimes when we talk when the garden is ablaze with gold in the late afternoon, the setting from a fairy tale, and Daniel appears more gnomelike than ever, he will say, as he has on many occasions at the age when repeating oneself is not unusual, "But how I remember stories from those books that brought princesses and heroes to me as I lay in the deep grass, goat bells tinkling softly as I read, swept away by words that changed my ragged clothes into palace finery." Then he relates one of those stories, and as some old and sensitive men do, those who have been through lives of heaven and hell, he will now and then start sobbing at the end of the tale. In seconds, he has been transformed from a seventy-year-old white-haired man who has known the Spanish Civil War into a boy whose recollection of childhood innocence, purity, and illusion would be enough to cause a stone to weep.

How many men or women have the good fortune to have a Kamante, Farah, or Dersu Uzala in their life? My existence has certainly been enriched by the presence of Daniel Gomez Caseró, who does not want me to leave this ranch and go to Africa. He does not say so with words, but with his eyes.

I squint and look out at the summer-scorched Spanish fields. Yellow background is the right color. Spanish pigs become wart hogs. Red-legged partridge call harshly from far sides of the pasture. Goats are transformed by blurred vision into Grant's and Thomson's gazelles, and the twisted oaks assume the layered and flat-top forms of yellow fever trees and thorntrees. What is it really going to be like?

July 29, Wednesday, 1:16 P.M., Cañada Grande
Last night went to sleep with unicorns roaming the dark places of my mind; awoke this morning with Africa at my side. Breathing softly, she lies close against me. Pull my hand from under the pillow and reach around to feel soft hair and familiar nose, cool to my touch as are her ears. Easing fingers along her side to her stomach, she sighs with pleasure of the caress.

Turn my head to look into eyes as deeply mascaraed as were, certainly, Cleopatra's. Stare into the depths of those soft, gazellelike orbs and think of her Africa, her roots. They were not pulled from the soil of Kenya and Tanzania's veldts and forests, where in three days I will be. Her source is the same as the Nile's, somewhere near the Mountains of the Moon, or to the north, on the southwestern Sudanese border in the country of the Zande, where Basenjis are known as Zande dogs.

In India, Jim Corbett kept a European spaniel and named it Robin. To Africa, Karen Blixen took a Russian dog and called it Dusk. Beryl Markham's bull terrier–English sheepdog mix was Buller. On the other hand, I live in Europe where I keep an African breed of dog and each has an African name: Kizzy, Kindu, and Toto. How the choice and naming of dogs speak of the people with whom they live.

Kizzy

11:45 P.M. Write from this familiar bed, this soft and quiet place to sleep, and think about the tent floor and ground that will replace it for the next three weeks. Take a photocopy of Springer's field journal from night table. Tomorrow I will be on the plane. Turn the copy of the faded and stained pages and read them again and again and again.

July 30, Thursday, 3:30 P.M., Iberia flight 322, Sevilla–Madrid
My consciousness is spinning with the aircraft engines. The plateau has been passed that accompanies most journeys, of the mind being on the way several days before the body actually departs for its destination.

139

Tonight I will spend in the Athens airport. Think of sitting ten hours there, waiting for the plane to Africa. How spoiled we've become. Rudolf Springer had taken months, and faced every kind of hardship, to reach Kenya. I will be there in twenty-four hours.

4:25 P.M., Barajas Airport, Madrid

A mosaic of waiting faces, some bright, some dull, all colors surround me. I know these faces, I've seen them a thousand times—they may have been my own.

8:27 P.M., Olympic flight 248, Madrid–Athens

"Somewhere below lies Naples," the pilot announces. Romulus and Remus transfix my mind as we fly over this country. Myth or reality? Boys suckled and raised by a she wolf, like Mowgli's adopted mother, Reksha. Does believing create reality? Fire walkers believe feet will not be burned by hot coals upon which they step. If there is such a thing as unicorns in the heart, can their existence in the mind be denied? Before an Italian proved otherwise, the earth was flat. Before Rudolf O. Springer invented his twenty-six-ingredient Approach Formula, who would have imagined that East African elephants, lions, and unicorns could be observed from distances as near as three inches, with no danger to the behavioralist?

July 31, Friday, 5:00 A.M., Athens Airport

Long night over. With coming light, names as romantic as unicorns flash, announcing passage to exotic places: Alexandria, Tel Aviv, Singapore.

11:30 A.M., Olympic flight 106, Athens–Nairobi

In-flight film begins. How ludicrous this seems when I try to imagine Rudolf Springer sometime in the 1880s, journeying from New York, via London, Lisbon, Tangier, Barcelona, Marseilles, Naples, and Alexandria on his way to Mombassa. What means of travel entertainment did he enjoy? Probably the simple act of trying to survive.

Star Trek: The Voyage Home. Normally would shut eyes, put on earphones to tune out film and into classical music channel. On screen is the name of good friend William Shatner to whom I've been unable to admit that I've never seen *Star Trek.*

Safe within Olympic Air 106, with its clean, white, portholed walls, flying through space. As the film progresses, I identify with Captain Kirk as much as I do with Springer. Not going to twentieth-century San Francisco, like Bill's ship—but also regressing in time, to the nineteenth-century Africa of romantic imagination. Instead of zooming along faster than sound to save two humpback whales, this mission is equally bizarre—attempting to encounter Hemingway's unicorn of Kilimanjaro, the animal thought to be nonexistent but documented by Springer 100 years ago.

1:30 P.M., Air Olympic flight 106, Athens–Nairobi

Twenty minutes and plane will be setting down in Nairobi, announces the pilot. From the aisle seat, strain to look out window. Ground visible and drawing closer. Cannot connect with the reality that below is Africa. Waited so long. Seen too many films. This must be a second feature: *My Voyage Home.*

Africa is down there.

A high wire fence surrounds the aerodrome—a wire fence and then a deep ditch. Where is there another aerodrome fenced against wild animals? Zebra, wildebeest, giraffe, eland—at night they lurk about the tall barrier staring with curious wild eyes into the flat field, feeling cheated.—Beryl Markham

2:40 P.M., Nairobi Airport

Customs and passport control. See Joe's face, bearded and smiling, in the crowd. Embrace. "Joe, I'm here, I'm in Africa," I repeat.

Once in the parking lot I hug Bill Wheeler and drop to the pavement to kiss the ground. "What are you trying to do," questions Bill, "get hepatitis, or any of a million awful diseases that infect that one square inch to which your lips were just pressed?" Excitement barely containable. Bill and Joe, having just returned to civilization from two-week foot safari to Olmoti and Embagai, are tired. Appear annoyingly lackadaisical.

"What about the unicorns?" I question. "Did you see any?"

"Only in the drawing you gave us to show the natives," Bill says with a tired smile.

"But you didn't even see any signs?" I question Joe. "Springer saw them there."

"Could be there," replies Joe. "It's just that we didn't have much time to do anything but get where we were going. Didn't see much of anything

Joe Sacerman

alive except beautiful forest, Masai, and flamingos. The place is so wild, animals run before you spot them. There was too much ground to cover. We had to go so far in such a short time. Didn't have time or energy to search out signs according to Springer's methods."

"Come on," beckons Bill. "Let's get going, we'll fill you in later."

My heart sinks. If Bill and Joe found no evidence of unicorns in two of the most remote areas of Tanzania, is there any chance at all of finding them in Kenya?

2:45 P.M., Elm Tree, road into Nairobi

Driving toward Nairobi, scenery distracts from the thought there may no longer be unicorns in East Africa. Too many things to see along the road, especially for eyes easily seduced by the tropically exotic.

As Elm Tree, "the vehicle of a gentleman," bounces along, Bill says, "We'll leave day after tomorrow for Amboseli and Kilimanjaro. Is there anything around here you'd like to see except Nairobi? Tomorrow we'll go downtown and stock up on fruit, vegetables, and stuff to eat."

"Before we set out," I answer, "I'd like to go to Karen Blixen's house."

"Can do that in the morning," says Bill. "You must be tired."

I must be tired, not having slept in twenty-four hours, but the excitement has dispersed fatigue. Tomorrow. Karen Blixen's house. Isak Dinesen's house. Denys Finch Hatton's house when not on safari. The house of "I had a farm in Africa." Could there be a more fitting place to start this quest?

5:20 P.M., Elm Tree, road into Nairobi center

Along the road, in fading light, ebony figures on a curio rack. Africans, alone and in groups, sit, kneel, squat; some stand, some stretch out on ground. Then at the edge of the highway, first African animal. A dead hyena. An omen?

"Did you see that?" asks Bill. "And if you're not sure you're in Africa, read the headline on that newspaper on the back seat." I pick up the July 31 copy of *The Nation:* WITCH DOCTOR'S DRINK KILLS FOUR VILLAGERS.

7:30 P.M., East Indian restaurant

Near the hotel dine at an East Indian restaurant where Bill and Joe tell me of their foot safari to Olmoti and Embagai. Long days of forced marches carrying sixty-pound backpacks; breathtaking scenery; thrill of having ventured where few white men have stepped; danger of continually being on Cape buffalo trails or crawling through their forest tunnels; very few animals seen (zebra, flamingos, and monkeys); a day spent at a morani [young warriors] meat camp.

Reports that absolutely no unicorn sightings or signs occurred during two weeks' walking in the same wild areas where Springer listed some of his most important discoveries are devastating to my morale.

9:45 P.M., Heron Court Hotel

In bed reflect: If Olmoti and Embagai had been exploited by white man for scientific and touristic reasons like the Serengeti and Nogorgongo, that might have explained my friends' failure to find even the slightest trace of unicorns in those craters, which have been frequented by few people except Masai living there in harmony with wild animals. Why had the Masai expressed no sign of recognition when shown the unicorn drawing by Bill and Joe? Rudolf Springer gathered material and explored this area barely three generations ago. Certainly, even if the animals had ceased to exist during the past fifty or sixty years, stories would have kept them alive in the minds of the Masai who today inhabit the crater highlands. The only thing that could explain, in part, the absence of *Unicornuus africanus* in this area are the tremendous numbers of Cape buffalo that Bill and Joe had not seen once, but heard crashing off through the brush and down tunnels and trails that had led my companions into the craters.

Relationship of unicorns to Cape buffalo had mystified Springer. The former, he wrote, seem to despise the latter. Does the present dense buffalo population indeed indicate the absence of unicorns in the two areas in Tanzania where one hundred years ago Springer wrote they had "flourished"? Unicorns—buffalo. Buffalo—unicorns . . . spiral into deep sleep.

August 1, Saturday, 8:35 A.M., Heron Court Hotel

Bird songs, exotic and undefinable, float through windows, assurance that this is not Spain or California. Doors slam, child cries, a toilet flushes, music—Brahms—all sounds of the Heron Court Hotel. Impatient to jump into khaki shorts, an old Spanish army shirt, and low, beaten, rough-looking walking boots, I put blue jeans, white tennis shoes, and polo shirt away for a month—that could be forever. This is a khaki country. The low "pip,ir,ee" of a white-browed robin chat is heard just outside the window.

9:45 A.M., Karen Blixen's house

A Masai child stares. I stand in Karen Blixen's garden, the Ngong Hills rising up behind us as she describes them: "The Mountain of Ngong stretches in a long ridge from North to South, and is crowned with four noble peaks like immovable dark blue waves against the sky." Feeling of space here as Karen Blixen wrote: "The views were immensely wide. Everything that you saw made for greatness and freedom, and unequalled nobility."

From the house, flowers cascade in flows of orange. Color everywhere (bougainvillea, thunbergia, lantana, quisqualis). Like Mexico, but here the eye is allowed to rest against the immensity of green landscape. House once in ruins, now restored by the Kenyan government, a ticket to imagination. Indoors smells of rich, dark old wood. Fresh day lilies placed in slim vases give feeling that Karen Blixen, the young, oval-faced woman of Africa, might momentarily step from the kitchen. Here there is not a trace of Isak Dinesen, the gaunt, mask-faced eccentric exiled in Denmark.

Sydney Pollack left film props behind when movie company abandoned Kenya. Bed is made. Ready for someone to slip into tonight. Over a chair drapes a khaki jacket topped by a safari hat. In bedroom, the gramophone horn carries Mozart through the air gently as the breeze that sways lace window curtains.

He also gave me my gramophone. It was a delight to my heart, it brought new life to the farm, it became the voice of the farm—"The soul within the glade the nightingale is."—Karen Blixen.

Figure blurs outside behind lace of curtains. Denys returned from shooting? Karen going to meet him? Time stops, then is turned back sixty-four years. Lovers, betrayed wife, unfaithful husband, faithful servants—Kamante and Farah—still inhabit these rooms as it is certain the unicorns inhabit the African wilderness where we will be in several days. I wonder about this house of Africa, and about an Africa before then—about Rudolf Springer's Kenya. Of Springer's scientific mind I know something. Of his heart? Nothing. Was there a Karen Blixen in his life? Of his private person there is no description, except for a great-great-niece's letter and the words "screwball uncle." Hardly a complimentary portrait, but one that might have been used to depict Karen Blixen—and other persons who have lived as they are instead of as society dictates they should be.

As I write these words Africa beckons with fragrance and sound. What place more fittng to start this quest for a noble Dark Continent and a noble, white, one-horned animal? Might Karen Blixen have sat here on the stone in front of her bedroom when she wrote: "Everything that you saw made for greatness and freedom, and unequalled nobility"?

Leaving the Bogani house, brilliant petals, sunbound, flake the wind. A flock of fire finches, cordon-bleus, and lavender finches fly to 、. . destinations as uncertain as my own?

11:30 A.M., Nairobi
Frontier town—underfoot and before eyes—back streets of downtown Nairobi. In boots, khaki shorts, and shirt, have never felt better in clothes or more comfortable..Could we be white hunters sixty years ago, come into Nairobi for provisions? Bill Wheeler, straw pith helmet shading his light blue eyes, strides ahead intently, followed by dark-bearded good-looking Joe and by me.

12:00 P.M., Nairobi market
Produce, flowers, food are sold in a central courtyard of ground floor. Curio shops line gallery of upper level. Crowded but quiet (unlike the deafening roar of Spanish markets, where everyone shouts). Even beggars, men with missing or twisted legs, who scoot about on their hands, plead with eyes and not voices. Yellow calla lilies, orange bird of paradise, red bird of paradise, chrysanthemums of all shades, nardos, yellow iris, purple status, day lilies seduce the nose, as everything, everywhere here, seduces the eyes.

1:30 P.M., Nairobi, downtown
Having seen extra space on top of the Land Rover and knowing that for the next two weeks I will not sleep as well in confines of a single-width sleeping bag on quarter-inch anti-humidity pad, I set out to buy a foam mattress and two blankets. Back streets jammed with saried East Indian women, turbaned and bearded Sikhs, bandanaed African girls, even a Masai, burnt-orange-robed and spear in hand, stands next to a Land Rover.

2:30 P.M., the Norfolk Hotel
Leave back streets and rough charm behind, lunch at the Lord Delamare Restaurant. Surrounded by tourists, our table could be in Marbella or Laguna Beach, except that here all waiters are black. Feel awkward in safari clothes.

3:30 P.M., Nairobi, downtown
Need to buy reference books, bird and mammal field guides. Go to a bookstore next to the New Stanley Hotel after which Joe and I wait on the corner for Bill, who has wandered off to look for a

Bill Wheeler

battery. It will power the electric fence that in the coming weeks hopefully will prevent baboons from destroying our frequently-to-be-left-alone tent.

If I felt awkward in khaki at Lord Delamare restaurant, here feel ridiculous. In front of us, there is a continual brown flow in and out of the New Stanley Hotel, a beige stream of tourists dressed in acrylic, right-out-of-the-box safari suits: telephone operators on vacation from New Jersey, factory workers on holiday from Liverpool. The men, feeling very much Alain Quartermain/Stewart Granger or Denys Finch Hatton/Robert Redford. The women, Deborah Kerr or Meryl Streep. Desire is overwhelming to flee this spot, to surface for air into the real Africa away from these pale people costumed as if going to a safari theme party.

August 2, Sunday, 5:00 A.M., foot of Ngong Hills
Now the quest begins on foot in the golden dawn of African dust. Will Rudolf O. Springer's *East African Elephant, Lion, and Unicorn Field Notes, Including Formula for Approaching the Above* 143

Listed Species at Distances up to Three Inches Without Danger to the Human Observer still be valid, though written a hundred years ago? Will Ernest Hemingway's inference that a unicorn exists on Kilimanjaro prove true, though spoken to me almost thirty years ago? I think in Africa anything is possible.

11:00 A.M., the Hardy House

Not far from Karen Blixen's house is another coffee farm of the same epoch—the Guy Hardy House. Have come to see Wheeler's friend, Bill McGill, a Scotsman of clear blue eyes. Joined in the kitchen by one of McGill's associates, Peter, a white Kenyan whose father was a professional hunter. When speaking of quest for unicorn, anticipate cynical smiles and jokes that such mention usually brings. But when I tell of experience with Hemingway, the searching leopard, and Kilimanjaro, Peter says, "Do you know that the two record elephant tusks were found 10,000 feet up on the mountain? Like with the leopard, nobody knows why he went to die there. Now the tusks, I think, are in the British Museum."

With a twinkle in his very blue eyes, Bill McGill then adds, "You know, if I were here looking for the Africa of your dreams and unicorns, there's only one place I'd go."

"The Ngurumans?" asks Peter.

"Right," Bill's face becomes serious but never so serious that his eyes don't sparkle. "It's the only virgin forest left in Kenya, not a tree's been cut there, and it's paradise on earth."

"No place as beautiful," continues Peter. "Got to be a bit careful though, there are some really nasty buffalo in there."

"Do tourists go there?" I question, excited because this is the same area that Springer mentioned repeatedly in his journal.

"Very few white people," answers Bill McGill. "There is a waterfall and a huge fig tree at a pond right out of a fairy tale—it was so lovely it made me want to cry."

"What you do is get a Masai that speaks English," suggests Peter, "some boys to carry your stuff. I'd go in from the Entaskera side, and walk through the forest to the edge of the Nguruman Escarpment, there you'll look across to Lake Natron and Tanzania. You can do it easily in two or three days."

"I want to try Kilimanjaro first because of Hemingway," I answer. "That's intriguing about those elephant tusks. If we don't find anything at Kilimanjaro, it's on to the Oloololo Escarpment. I have a hunch that the wildebeest migration from the Serengeti, once it crosses Masai Mara, stops at the escarpment because unicorns are on the top."

"Try it," smiles Bill McGill. "But if your unicorns are anywhere, it's the Ngurumans."

"Why Hemingway would suggest Kilimanjaro from the Amboseli side," said Peter, stroking his beard, "doesn't make sense. You've got to go into Tanzania to climb it; go to Marangu where the walks are organized, it'll take you five days, about eighty kilometers there and back. It's all very well organized with guides and nice huts where you'll spend the night. It's a good climb, a high one, 5,800 meters. As someone once said, nothing lives on the summit, but just below the snow line, below the no-life line, there's a point at which a few sparse grasses represent the dawn of life itself."

"Forget Kilimanjaro and the Oloololo Escarpment," smiles McGill. "The Ngurumans is the place. It's where you're going to see wild animals in the true sense of the word. That is if they let you see them. Natural tendency is to run from man—except some of the solitary buffalo. And you won't see another white face until you come out."

"Do you know how far the migration is into Masai Mara?" questions Bill Wheeler.

"I was down there the other day," answers McGill, " and they're just around Keekerok, I don't think they've gotten to Governor's Camp yet."

"So we won't see a river crossing," I ask. (Supposedly one of the most spectacular wildlife spectacles on earth occurs when tens of thousands of wildebeest and zebra gather on the north bank of the river and then suddenly decide to cross. A charcoal wave of antelope traverses the muddy Mara, wildebeest leaping from fifty-foot ledges into the water, heads and horns surging through dust and foam before they reach the far bank.)

"I think it's going to be a while," said Bill McGill.

"Listen, Robert," says Peter. "If you truly feel this way about the real Africa and want to avoid tourists—when you go to Amboseli [he focuses on Bill Wheeler], don't take the main road, that's crazy with minibuses of tourists flying over the blacktop at seventy miles per hour. Bill [Wheeler], there's a dirt pipeline road that will get Robert right into Africa. Here, let me draw you a map."

12:30 P.M., Elm Tree, Athi Plains, Pipeline Road
Elm Tree rattles along. Eyes can't look in enough directions at same time. Feel like a street person who, accustomed to rummaging through garbage can for bread crust, suddenly encounters a table piled with every color and fragrant kind of enticing tropical food imaginable.

1:00 P.M. Stop on top of hill overlooking Athi Plains.

This was the stillness of the eternal being, the world as it had always been.—Carl Jung

Cattle fleck far off ocher slopes. Not the Herefords or Angus from childhood California, nor the black fighting bulls of a young manhood in Spain; these are exotic Masai beasts with horns as long and big around as my legs. Here even domestic bovines seem cast from aesthetic molds.

A flight of superb starlings flashes metalic blue overhead. On a far ridge graze four Thomson's gazelles.

And now the whole of Africa lies before you with open arms, proud and grateful for your love. The wind, the sun, the shade, the great mango trees, the black children, the game in the Reserve, the white peak of Kilimanjaro and your own Ngong Hills, when you see them . . . all of them say "Welcome, welcome"; and you are riding straight into the open heart of Africa.—Karen Blixen

1:50 P.M. Now, twenty-one miles out of Nairobi. First zebra herd. Five graze, two involved in mutual grooming, three doze facing into wind. Stallion stands sentry 100 feet away from harem. Cori bustard, largest of flying birds, walks afield, intently following a course that will lead him where? Weaverbird nests ornament acacia trees. First ostrich.

2:15 P.M. Cape buffalo!—James Michener was right. Cape buffalo are the most unpredictable, murderous animals in Africa. Even Springer's formula would not work with them. Still I love them. The death they represent makes one feel more vital in their presence. Red-billed oxpecker hisses,

"tssssss," and chatters shrilly as it flies from buffalo's forehead. Club-tailed *Charaxes* butterflies abundant.

2:37 P.M., Pipeline Road
No doubt. First look at where I always wanted to be but never was. East African waterhole exhibit at L.A. County Museum of Natural History dazzles eyes as it did more times than I can remember. Small boy in the darkness of the great hall, peering through glass, imagining that any moment longdead, dusty stuffed animals would suddenly come to life. Now I am in a Land Rover. Animals before me are moving. Grass is swaying with the breeze. Hides are sleek and shiny. Eyelids open and close. And there is sound. Seven zebra directly in front. Four off to one side. Wildebeest to right. Four to the left. Six ostrich dance back and forth in chorus. Mixed herd of twenty Thomson's and Grant's gazelles.

Ask Bill to stop Elm Tree. Open door. Softened by overcast sky, landscape stretches out, alive and vibrant on all sides, not dull painted background at L.A. County Museum. Animals and birds alert, watching us. Wildebeest warn with warped bullfrog croaks. Zebra signal with sharply echoed barks. I jump out of Elm Tree and sprint toward zebra. Push off, feet into grass. First burst of speed, for a few seconds, allows me to join flight over the rolling hills. I am in Africa! I am in Africa! I am alive!

Antelope, ostrich, and zebra have so far outdistanced me that I stop, as do they, maintaining flight distance.

Intoxicated with excitement of moment, flop into grass and gaze up at billows of clouds. Small, orange butterfly (common acraea) glides over brow that is caressed by long veldt grass. Am now completely out of sight. Bill and Joe must think me insane.

3:00 P.M., Pipeline Road
Spot three cow giraffe, each with calf. Land Rover leaves road. Stop so I can climb up on overhead rack. Distant memory warns that Ylla, photographing a bullock race in India, was killed—catapulted from the hood of a car that struck a hole. Land Rover lunges ahead, swerving to avoid warthog burrows, camouflaged by tall grass. Hands grip to knuckle whiteness pipe of luggage rack. Wind rush 145

in face. Animals rise and fall in syrupy strides, buoyant as ducks, long-necked as swans, limpid-eyed as does, spotted as leopards—beautiful as giraffes.

3:37 P.M., *Highway A104 to Amboseli*

Leave dirt road and lurch onto blacktop of highway to Amboseli. Driving south, yellow fever trees fan out against dark red-orange earth, same color as terrain in other parts of the world where, almost without exception, unicorns were found.

Smash! A Jackson's hornbill smacks the windshield, wedges against glass and rain wiper. Stop. Joe removes the bird. Examine it. Where there are motor vehicles, life is fragile for hornbills—and for us. Drive on, silenced by the death of this lovely black-and-white, red-billed African bird. Another bad omen?

3:40 P.M. Speed along. Spot a pair of Fisher's turacos in the top of a fever tree. Bill and Joe seem not to notice them, nor any of the other birds, unless big as vultures, that color and glide the passing landscape. Sinking feeling. Might they not have had the patience or perception to have sighted unicorns or signs of them in Olmoti and Embagai craters? During ten-day foot safari, they did not see one buffalo in a forest dense with buffalo. Admittedly, animals of that almost virgin wilderness are wary and difficult to spot. Bothers me to imagine that unicorns, inhabitants of Embagai and Olmoti, do not exist where we will search during coming month at the red-circled places on our map—Kilimanjaro, Oloololo Escarpment, Loita Hills, Nguruman Escarpment.

3:50 P.M. Impala, most graceful of creatures, even more so than the single-horned, white animal focal point of this safari, bound the landscape where now the Masai also appear. Many Masai have changed handsome solid-color red or leather-orange body togas for plaid fabrics more in tone with Scottish highlands than with Kenya.

4:12 P.M. Flock of half a hundred Kenyan crested guinea fowl scatters and breaks into the brush. Smaller and bluer-headed than domestic guineas. Terrain changing. Earth even redder. Fever trees more frequent. Joe drives. Bill plays flamenco on guitar to take me back to the country from which I have come and not the one where I am and want to be.

4:30 P.M., *Namanga*

Have stopped in Namanga, last village before Amboseli, to check the loss of gear fluid, a chronic problem with Elm Tree. Down a quart.

6:15 P.M., *Amboseli Gate*

Gate to the reserve closes at six. With "Jambo" and smile we enter. Behind dusty trail the sun is halved by a purple bank of clouds. Shout to Bill to halt the Land Rover so that I can photograph first sunset in the bush. "You're not supposed to get out of the car in the reserves," he cautions, "only at the campsite."

"Then it is going to be like some safari park in America," I say, feeling inhibited already and removed from Africa. Elm Tree's engine noises shut out other sound, and gas fumes mask perfumed countryside. Thirty-eighty kilometers to campsite flashes by a sign in the going light.

Kilimanjaro is somewhere ahead, protected from sight by brewing cumulus. Could the view of the mountain itself be more glorious than the one that dazzles our eyes? A setting pleading for a unicorn.

7:30 P.M., *Amboseli Reserve*

Wildebeest eyes gleam like mica from walls of some deep, dark prehistoric cave through which Elm Tree seems to be moving. Tree stumps uproot the landscape. Bomb-blasted from the soil or ripped up by some devastating flood? What happened here? "Elephant damage," replies Bill. "They're knocking down all of the trees in Amboseli, turning it into an immense grassland."

8:00 P.M. Arrive at campsite. Search for place to pitch the tent. Headlights pick up a herd of impala, scurrying like autumn leaves before Elm Tree's approach. Fresh elephant dung everywhere.

8:25 P.M. Tent up. Fire blazes. Eighty feet away branches crack and tree sways, as if shook by a hurricane. Whipped by the wind, campfire flames blaze orange the tusks of an elephant ripping limbs from acacia tree.

11:15 P.M. Wind surges and subsides, both bringing with it and masking sound. Before going to bed, take a flashlight and try and get a better look at the bull elephant, which extends ears and trunk when Bill approaches to within sixty feet.

August 3, Monday, 2:15 A.M., *camp, Amboseli*

Can't sleep. Don't want to miss single sound this first night. Apprehensive. Only a slim piece of

nylon tenting separates us from the animals behind those noises.

3:30 A.M., tent, Amboseli

Mind jumps thought-to-thought, everything but sleep. Have I based too much on Hemingway's leopard?

John Reader's *Kilimanjaro* mentions Hemingway and the leopard. Switch on flashlight and pull recently purchased book from bag. Turn to index and see "Hemingway, Ernest 35, *The Snows of Kilimanjaro* 44, 57." On page 35, Reader describes his own climb:

The peak seems to retreat as you cross the northwest ridges, and the ice seemed much farther away. But Kenya was very close. Glistening tin roofs indicated the position of Loitokitok, the border town from where Ernest Hemingway must frequently have glazed up at Kilimanjaro while he was an honorary game warden based there in the early 1950s. I could just make out the line of the Chyulu Hills, from where my wife and I had caught a memorable glimpse of Kilimanjaro in 1976. I could see the Amboseli Swamp, and the lookout hill we used to climb every morning to see where the elephants were. But most of Kenya was obscured by cloud.

Why, again, I pondered, had Hemingway said I would see the unicorn from the Kenyan side? Our campsite, according to Bill, isn't more than a mile from the lookout hill that Reader mentions. And why hadn't Reader, scaling Kilimanjaro on numerous occasions, exploring it from one side to the other, the ash crater itself, the glaciers, even the site of the "dried and frozen carcass of a leopard," seen even a trace of unicorns? I turn to page 44:

We were camped under Leopard Point, as I have said, but although the name was familiar enough to him, Simon [Reader's guide] had never heard the legend that Ernest Hemingway had immortalized in *The Snows of Kilimanjaro*. And when I

explained that sometime in the 1920s the frozen corpse of a leopard had been discovered on the rocks above us, Simon expressed incredulity. Why would it have climbed up there? he asked. And when I told him I intended to climb up and look for the remains of the creature, he expressed amusement. If a cow had been left there only seven years before, did I expect there would be any recognizable remains of it there now? he asked.

Nonetheless, I climbed up and scoured not just Leopard Point but the entire ridge from Gillman's Point to Hans Meyer Notch. I found three rusty cans containing paraffin cached among the rocks and, on a level space under the highest rocks of Leopard Point, a tea-tray-sized piece of galvanized zinc. Nothing was written on it, though a hole in the centre suggested that it had once been fixed to something and perhaps had carried a message. Probably it had marked the spot where the leopard had been found once the creature itself had disappeared entirely. There is ample proof of the leopard's existence to be found in photographs and published reports of the day, some of which suggest the manner of its disappearance. Dr Reusch, the local missionary who first discovered the relic, once cut off an ear as a souvenir. He would have preferred to take the entire head, he wrote, but found the corpse too dry and frozen for easy dismemberment.

"No one has explained what the leopard was seeking at that altitude," wrote Hemingway. No, but whatever ambition had driven the creature to such a lifeless landscape of shale and ice, I thought while sitting there, it had found a primeval place beyond which no living thing can proceed.

In the photographic section of his book, Reader includes a sepia print of the distorted and frozen leopard with two women and this caption: "Above, the leopard immortalized by Ernest Hemingway in *The Snows of Kilimanjaro*, photographed in 1926 with nurses from the Lutheran Mission at Marangu."

By nature unicorns avoid heavily populated tourist areas—as I am finding the real Africa does also. Does this connect with Hemingway: "I guarantee you'll see it from the Amboseli side, and you don't have to climb the mountain."

August 3, Monday, 4:30 A.M., tent, Amboseli

I awaken sweating from anxious dreams of a vanishing Africa, being witness to an exodus of animals that will never return. The unicorn is swirled in the mists of Kilimanjaro, then disappears—forever. Sounds of dark Africa rescue me from this nightmare.

Right next to tent, warthogs grunting, the patter and pounding of an impala stampede. What frightened them? Lion? Leopard, listening to us breathing inside of the flimsy spiderweb of protection? For sure, my heart, at a hundred yards, can be heard pounding. Then comes another noise, a deep rumbling one that as a child often heard, in the elephant tent of Ringling Brothers and Barnum & Bailey circus. The tusker has moved so close to us that I can hear his stomach gurgling.

5:00 A.M. First traces of dawn bring faint light to this blue protective cocoon of a tent. Africa is outside! Unzip mosquito netting and tent flap. Sun seems still an hour from appearing, and in the coming blue-gray light all that can be seen of Kilimanjaro is the base. Mountaintop remains behind clouds.

Anxious to see the promised glory of Kilimanjaro, its ice-crowned summit tinted coral in the rays of the rising sun!—H.K. Binks

6:05 A.M. Two Masai accompany the sun as it rises from behind a hill. Not far away, a zebra mare stands with her new foal. Here man and beast live in harmony. At the sight, my heart rises with the dawn. A tribe of Kenyan crested guinea fowl salute the morning with a harsh series of "tuks" followed by softer clicking notes.

6:30 A.M. camp, Amboseli

Luck! Bank of clouds opens, one layer parting behind another, to reveal the mountain's snowcap but little else.

"What did you expect?" asks Bill. "And how do you propose to look for . . . for your unicorns?"

Trouble is, don't know where to start or how to answer him.

James, a young Masai camp guard friend of Bill's, appears. After greetings and introductions, I sketch a unicorn on a page in this notebook. "Have you ever seen an animal like this? I question. "Like a zebra, but with one horn on its head."

James studies the drawing carefully before answering, "No, I have never seen anything here like that animal."

While Bill and James talk of a short foot safari they once did together, I walk to a tree an elephant had toppled the night before. Kilimanjaro's snowcap is now rosied by the rising sun. In foreground, like miniature figures in a Brueghel painting, copper-coated impala graze before a stand of acacias that cuts dark forms against pale blue of distant mountain's base. Only now can I grasp the full meaning of Peter Matthiessen's description:

At 19,340 feet, Kilimanjaro is the highest solitary mountain in the world. Mt. Kenya is a shard of rock thrust upward from the earth, but Kilima Njaro, the White Mountain, has ascended into the sky, a place of religious resonance for tribes all around its horizons.

The glacier glistens. A distant snowpeak scours the mind, but a snowpeak in the tropics draws the heart to a fine shimmering painful point of joy.

6:45 A.M. James smiles. His teeth sparkle of Masai manhood, as he says good-bye to Bill. "James," I question, "do you know what Kilimanjaro means?"

"Kilimanjaro means 'the White Mountain,'" he says slowly. "At least that is what I understand it to mean."

Have you ever heard it called 'the House of God'?" I ask.

"I have never heard it called that, but perhaps it is by some people."

When James has left, some trace of memory causes me to again look at the inside cover of the Matthiessen book. *See Ol Doinyo Lengai, page 2."* Flip through book:

. . . a remote volcano known to the Masai as *ol doinyo le eng ai*, the Mountain of God, called commonly "Lengai . . ." To the eastward, far beyond the far end of the valley, the Mountain of God rose for a long moment in the swirling clouds, then vanished. The Maasai say that Lengai or Ngai moved to this place in the sky after a Dorobo hunter shot an arrow at him, and most of the day for most of the year his realm is hidden; now Ngai is remote, beyond their reach, and they are visited by death and famine . . . In 1967, this last active volcano of the Crater Highlands erupted, shrouding its slopes and all the country around with fine gray ash.

In the five-line prologue to *The Snows of Kilimanjaro*, Ernest Hemingway writes of Kilimanjaro: "Its western summit is called the Masai Ngaje Ngai, the House of God." Why did he confuse or substitute Kilimanjaro for Lengai?

Later, when Matthiessen climbed partway up Lengai he found seemingly fossilized rhinoceros tracks high on the mountain. He wrote, "Holding a hoofprint in my hands, I raised my eyes to where that rhinoceros had taken form in the poisonous clouds and rushed down the fiery ridge. What had drawn it up into the mists? Had it been blind, like the buffalo found in the snow high on Mt. Kenya?"

Could the leopard of Kilimanjaro and the elephant whose immense tusks were found there, also have been blind? Then, perhaps the leopard was not seeking anything in the snow, just a place to die.

Piping, drumming, trumpeting. Hornbills, tambourine doves, wood pigeons, guineas, glossy starlings, waxbills, rollers, mousebirds, fishing eagles, spurfowl chorus to bring me out of my thoughts while Kilimanjaro stands still as a painted backdrop.

"Robert," calls Bill from the now blazing campfire, "have you decided where you want to start looking?"

"Don't know," I answer. "Now I feel wrong about this place. Remembering what Matthiessen wrote, I can't help but think maybe, if unicorns are on a mountain, it would be Lengai, and not here. Still, I can't explain what Hemingway told me or why he confused one mountain for the other."

"Look," suggests Joe, "why don't we just get going and maybe something will come to you. Remember those forest unicorns you had given up on in Idaho? We just scratched around until we found them."

"Sounds right," says Bill. "We'll drive the reserve this morning, have lunch at the lodge, and do some photography this afternoon. Then you can decide if you want to stay on or move out to Masai Mara."

9:00 A.M. I feel insignificant in this country of vast landscapes and immense beasts. And more confused than ever by Hemingway's allusion to a unicorn on Kilimanjaro. Discouraged, after two hours of pondering and staring, I turn my back on the mountain; "white as fresh snow and larger than life," where could his unicorn be?

9:30 A.M., Elm Tree, Amboseli
Near camp, movement catches my eye. Two dik-dik feeding. Beyond them a bull elephant browses a hundred yards off the road.

"Let's go see him," I say.

"But he's off the road," answers Bill. "Can't leave the road in the reserve."

"But that looks like a road," I motion toward tracks made by tires or perhaps by an elephant dragging branches.

"Could be," smiles Bill.

Drive within fifty yards of bull and stop. Continues to feed, not taking notice of us. I slide open the Land Rover window. "I can turn around a bit so you can get a better shot," volunteers Bill.

"Wait, I don't want to shoot," I say, and cupping my hands out from my mouth, give the repeated cough-roar with which a male lion finishes his call. Elephant's veined ears, gray and immense, flare in the sun, trunk up, trumpets. Charges! Bill guns Elm Tree to leave the tusker behind, slashing the clouds of dust with his ivory. Adrenaline ignites my senses with excitement as I question what will happen in ten days outside the reserve, and with completely wild elephants. What will happen when I test Springer's Approach Formula and body oil?

12:00 P.M. Spurfowl flashes across road, beyond which a gray tidal wave of dust sweeps toward us, seemingly supported by slim columns of whirlwinds to curtain Kilimanjaro from view.

3:00 P.M. Cruise park roads. Bill and Joe seek lions and rhinos. I care only, apart from unicorns, about my favorite of African animals, the Cape buffalo. But don't find lions, or rhinos, or buffalo, just white tour bus after tour bus, photographing elephants and zebra that stand along the roads like dairy cattle, calmly chewing grass.

Fortunately, dust storm becomes intense enough to drive the tourists back to the lodge. Sun setting through the curtain of dust will make for dramatic photographs.

5:00 P.M. Road dead-ends at flat dryness of Amboseli Lake stretching boundaryless into the dust. Light will not be really good for another hour and a half. Bill stops the Land Rover, and with binoculars I scan horizon. "Kew-koo-wah, kew-koo-wah," call a trio of scaly francolins as they run off to roost. Suddenly, there is a shape. A blur of gray in the distance. Coming through fog of earth particles that swirl above dry lake. Shape approaching closer, but not close enough to identify. Too large to be a zebra, or Cape buffalo. Coming faster, and smaller than an elephant. Binoculars pick up sharpness of the horn, cutting through the haze like a shark fin at sea. A rhinoceros! Immense black rhino, running intently, alert and seeming bothered, now dominates the scene, head held high, like some prehistoric monster. Moves parallel to Elm Tree, then turns in our direction.

Where is this beast coming from, so determined in his direction? Where is he going? What reason for his anger? Now rhino coming straight at Land Rover. Bill starts motor and shoves gear stick into reverse and we shoot backward to give great dark shape a wide exit across the road. How could anyone have ever mistaken a rhinoceros for a unicorn? Rhino has crossed over, and disappears into the swirls of gray to recall Peter Matthiessen's experience high near the summit of Lengai: "Imagine the sight of that dark thing in the smoke of the volcano; had an African seen it, the rhino might have become a beast of legend."

8:00 P.M. Sun is down. Strings of wildebeest and zebra walk across the flat golden-purple expanse. An African exodus? The dusk of an epic. Now all of the tourists are safe inside lodge, exchanging tallies of animals seen during whirl around park, and we are bumping along through the darkness that laces reality with fantasy and sets free the imagination as Kipling set free his Bat:

> Now, Chill the kite brings home the night
> That Man the Bat sets free.
> This is the hour of pride and power,
> Talon and tusk and claw
> Oh, hear the call! Good hunting all
> That keep the Jungle Law!

8:15 P.M. Stop to gather firewood in the blackness. Before bending over to pick up a dry log, shine flashlight, panning surrounding bushes with little chance of seeing a predator.

A topi gallops off, accompanied by the thunderheads that leave Kilimanjaro and the sky clear tonight, but my mind clouded with the riddle and prospect of defeat. What, in truth, was Hemingway's leopard searching for, its eyes blazing like the star-streaked African sky overhead?

10:15 P.M. James appears with Masai friend. Five of us sit close around fire. Wind cold. Conversation spaced with moments of silence. "Chucker, chucker, chucker, chucker," comes the liquid call of the Nubian nightjar.

Superficial talk floats like smoke from the log that Joe has thrown on the coals. Bill brushes teeth. Toothpaste foams mouth and whitens beard like froth on the fur of a rabid animal. Masai laugh.

Log is reduced to embers. Pauses between talk are long. Words closer to the bone. "It is strange that so many people come here to see the animals," slowly says James. "They come here, and the animals are their only interest. But what can a buffalo tell you? What can a zebra tell you? They cannot tell you one thing. But the people who come here do not want to talk with our people. And our people have many things to say and to teach to others."

"Then, tell me something," I say. "Of all of the animals, which is the most dangerous?"

"The buffalo," he answers.

"More than the lion?"

"A lion will not attack you, usually, unless you force him to do so. Neither will an elephant. A buffalo will attack you for no reason. He is like the devil who does evil for the sake of doing evil."

"Then how do you kill a buffalo?" asks Bill. "How do the morani kill a buffalo?"

"It is not legal to hunt in Kenya today," answers James. "You cannot do it."

"Come on, James," smiles Bill. "Don't tell me that when a bunch of morani get together and drink a little pombe beer that they don't still hunt."

James's sharply filed and separated teeth gleam as he grins, "Well, occasionally it is done. But buffalo are bad, very bad. Often there will be one in a place and no Masai can go near that place, because the buffalo will try to kill anyone who comes near his place. Sometimes he kills several people and injures many others."

"Then how do you kill him?" Bill repeats.

"We spear him," answers James. "We kill him with spears."

"That must be very dangerous," says Bill, the flickers of flame reflected in his eyeglasses.

James smiles.

"You must be very brave," smiles Joe.

James grins but does not answer.

Sit. A quarter of an hour of silence. James and his friend stand up. "It is time for us to disappear," says James, and they do so into the night.

"Wee-woo, wee-woo,"—the low but far-carrying voice of a pearl-spotted owlet.

August 4, Tuesday, 7:33 A.M., Amboseli

Bill and Joe finish breakfast. Tell them that we should push on to Masai Mara. To stay in Amboseli longer is a waste of time. Hemingway's unicorn will have to remain either a mystery or a joke.

Leave the camp and sadly walk several hundred yards toward Kilimanjaro, then stop, lean against a stump, and put the binoculars to my eyes. Clear sky. A longtailed fiscal shrike calls harshly and ends call with clear whistle. For one last time recall Ernest Hemingway's words: "I can guarantee that if you approach Mount Kilimanjaro from the Amboseli side, and you don't have to climb the mountain, you'll see a unicorn at its summit. White as fresh snow, larger than life, and . . ."

Field glasses zoom in on snowcap. See not mountain, only a white shape against blue. Two white legs! The curve of the white stomach! The extension of the white neck with head and horn out of view, to the left, resting on the out-of-sight summit! Hemingway's unicorn! The reason for his smile! A white-snow unicorn spreads out on the mountaintop.

Run back to camp! "Bill! Joe! Look! Take the binoculars! The summit of the mountain. Forget that it's a mountain! Forget that its snow! What do you see? What shape?"

Bill grabs binoculars and clanks them excitedly against his spectacles. "It's . . . it's the shape of a white animal with its legs stretching downward," he says. "It's lying down. Yeah, I see what you mean. Robert, now I'll never be able to look at Kilimanjaro without seeing that."

"He told me it was white as snow and bigger than life," I explain. "He was talking about something larger than the real beast."

"Then there's not a unicorn on Kilimanjaro," Joe says.

"There is, look through the glasses," I hand them to him. "Haven't we been reading that the glaciers are melting, the snow is recessing every year? Look at this park. Where there were forests, now it looks like a dusty battlefield. Don't you see what's being done to this planet? We're messing up the atmosphere, causing the ice to melt. Destroying the environment, pushing the animals toward existing only in books."

"But where does the unicorn come in?" questions Bill, for the first time vaguely serious when he mentions the animal.

"Hemingway wasn't playing a joke," I exclaim. "We aren't going to leave Amboseli without having seen his unicorn—not Springer's animal of fur and flesh—but a unicorn nonetheless. What does the unicorn represent? Beauty and purity—nature. And the Kilimanjaro one is a unicorn that anyone can see. Stop now while there is barely time. If you destroy it, you destroy yourselves! Man is lost when he's lost touch with nature, with the reason for his being."

Silence as we stand staring at the mountain. Even without the binoculars, obviously snow flows form a white animal, stretched out on the mountaintop, hind legs to the right, forelegs to the left, neck extended, and head out of view to the left. Finally I question, "Is that what it is or not?"

"That's what it looks like," admits Bill.

"Now that you point it out, that's what I see," agrees Joe.

"But then what about the real thing?" questions Bill, the cynical smile having returned to his lips."

"Don't worry!" I shout. "If we found this one, then finding one in the flesh is next, and it's going to be at the top of the Oloololo Escarpment."

9:13 A.M., Elm Tree, Amboseli

Elm Tree also seems anxious, as loaded and groaning we leave the campsite. "Where do the reserve boundaries end?" I ask Bill.

"Over by those trees." He motions with his head to a stand of acacias a quarter of a mile away. "It cuts in there. Why?"

"As soon as we cross the line or where the boundary should be," I answer, "let's stop. I want to step back into Africa again. I want to see Kilimanjaro, but as a participant, not as a spectator. I don't want to see it from a movie screen, or from a car—I want to see it from Africa."

9:30 A.M. Elm Tree's motor is turned off. We climb out, feet blossom in dust, making contact, becoming part of the landscape. Now the voice of this country. "Guttar, guttar, guttar, guttar," clucks a chestnut-bellied sand grouse, followed by the weak plaintive "tsee, tsee," of a yellow-bellied eremomelia, sounds that were indistinguishable from within the Land Rover. Warm sun on skin. Fragrances of plants and earth and insects. "Swish" of our boots through the grass. Pause to gather wild flowers, which I press into journal.

Kilimanjaro looms ahead, the unicorn now so obviously at its summit. A herd of impala that took no notice of Elm Tree brings up heads at sight, sound, and smell of other beings—ourselves. Now on foot, out of the vehicle, we are creatures to be reckoned with; to whom they must relate. In long bounding leaps they arc between two acacia trees that frame mountain. Feeling of insignificance invades me. I stare up at Kilimanjaro. What was Hemingway's leopard searching for on the mountain? Perhaps, like me, for itself.

11:47 A.M., Elm Tree, Lake Amboseli

Flat, white, and dry stretches Lake Amboseli, flooded in heat waves, shimmering, transforming, and reflecting shapes that venture onto it. What is moving out there? A file of dark figures . . . Masai? In the tide of heat waves, legs become longer. "Unicorns?" asks Joe, having been with me on previous desert expeditions. We squint and strain eyes through binoculars and telephoto lenses. Shapes take form. Wildebeest.

12:00 P.M. Pair of eagles zooms low over cracked earth. A hare leaps up. They chase. Hare zigzags in search for cover. Eagle hits and topples him. Seems no hope for hare. Again on his feet, reaches cover of bush. Eagles glide low and frustrated overhead.

12:15 P.M. New shapes wade the mirage. Trio of giraffe, minute figures through the binoculars, take form. Long legs lost in white heat waves.

2:15 P.M., Namanga

Pull out our crate of food and eat while Elm Tree has its muffler welded. Here, at the garage, are other white travelers, other Land Rovers. The same questions. Where have you been? What have you seen? Where are you gong? The animals they name we have heard a dozen times in these few days in Africa. The animal in our thoughts, the unicorn, remains unmentioned. What creatures have these persons really seen through the distortion of camera and binocular lens? From the distortion of their minds?

Remote from nature, and living by complicated artifice, man in civilization surveys through the glass of his knowledge and sees thereby a feather magnified and the whole image in distortion. We patronize them for their incompleteness, their tragic fate of having taken form so far below ourselves. And therein we err, and greatly err. For the animal shall not be measured by man. In a world older and more complete than ours they move finished and complete, gifted with extensions of the senses we have lost or never attained, living by voices we shall never hear. They are not brethren, they are no underlings; they are other nations, caught with ourselves in the net of life and time, fellow prisoners of the splendour and travail of the earth.—Henry Beston

5:15 P.M., pond next to highway

Color changes landscape. Pass red-orange pond. Faint glimmer of recognition. Some anxious magnetism causes me to ask Bill to stop Elm Tree, turn back, and drive off the road to the pond.

The soil and water warmly hued by disappearing sun. Yellow fever trees rise and spread about like vegetation from a fairy tale. Then comes the sound. A loud, far-carrying "har, har, har." My heart pauses! Long drawn-out, ravenlike, catlike. A cry the description of which I have read a hundred times in Springer's journal—the call of a Hadada ibis.

"That's it!" I shout to Bill and Joe. Fifty yards away the bird sits on the low branch of a fever tree. I walk, slowly, closer. Bird cries again and takes to wing, feathers glistening in metallic flashes of green, black, and purple. Alights on the ground forty yards away from us. I walk nearer. Allows me to approach within fifty feet before again taking to air. Bill and Joe have run back to Elm Tree for their cameras.

Ibis slowly circles water, then lands on dead branch. Seems to be slowly leading me around pond. Bill and Joe are back, focusing telephoto lens.

Ibis suddenly cries repeatedly, flashes into the sky, upward, circles pond three times, far-carrying voice sounding each time he passes overhead, then holds straight course northwest—in the direction of the Oloololo Escarpment. Bill smiles as if to say, "Another coincidence." And I can't resist saying, "You'll see."

August 5, Wednesday, 7:00 A.M., Bill McGill's house, Karen, Nairobi

Spend night at Bill McGill's house. Awaken clean, the dust showered out of us night before by icy water (unfortunately, the upstairs water heater had not been turned on). Joe has bad rash on right side, waist, and buttock. Lymph nodes swollen. Bill and I concerned.

12:05 P.M. Question future of this journal:

There are as many Africas as there are books about Africa—and as many books about it as you could read in a leisurely lifetime. Whoever writes a new one can afford a certain complacency in the knowledge that his is a new picture agreeing with no one else's, but likely to be haughtily disagreed with by all those who believe in some other Africa.—Beryl Markham

4:15 P.M. Leave Bill McGill's house and bounce along road to Masai Mara. Karen Blixen was loved here. The neighborhood called Karen. There is a Karen school, a Karen hospital, a Karen store.

7:45 P.M., Elm Tree, road to Masai Mara

At last reach the bottom of Rift Valley. Sun setting. Kongoni crosses road. Decide to look for campsite instead of pushing on into night and having to set up tent in darkness at Masai Mara Talek River gate.

August 6, Thursday, 3:00 P.M.

First view of Oloololo Escarpment. Place where the great migration turns back and where over a hundred years ago only the unicorn ventured beyond distant rise of purple on the horizon. Like the quagga—has the unicorn also disappeared from the face of Africa? Smoke rises from beyond the escarpment. Summer fires or signals of angry gods? Quarter of a mile in front of Elm Tree runs a Masai child, red cloth blowing like bird wings in breeze, arm extended high, holding a fine green vine, trailing it behind him like the tail of a kite. Dashes across road and into a stand of acacia. Here one moment, brilliant and magical, then in an instant gone—like Africa.

4:00 P.M., Talek River Gate

Set up camp next to Talek River, outside and a mile down from reserve gate. Riverbanks beyond tent worn deep with buffalo trails. "Graak, graak, graak," from brush at the water's edge—the grating call of yellow-necked spurfowl.

8:15 P.M. Hyenas chorus, whooping from opposite riverbank.

There are so many hyenas about . . . at night; I have become really fond of their long howls and screams, that are part of Africa . . .—Karen Blixen

August 7, Friday, 3:30 A.M., tent

Awakened by lion roar-sigh. The nylon, thin side of the tent flaps against my face, beyond it is the lion and the African night. Now too awake to return to sleep. Hyenas whoop. Nightjar cries. Moon brightens tent top. Wind comes spreading, stronger, like wave after wave through the trees along the river.

9:43 A.M., Masai Mara, Elm Tree

As we crest hill, herds numbering thousands of wildebeest and zebra string across the landscape, some in groups, others single file like lines of black insects against ocher landscape. Elm Tree soon surrounded by croaking gnus and barking zebra.

As the herd moved it became a carpet of rust-brown and grey and dull red. It was not like a herd of cattle or of sheep, because it was wild, and it carried with it the stamp of wilderness and the freedom of a land still more a possession of Nature than of men. To see ten thousand animals untamed and not branded with the symbols of human commerce is like scaling an unconquered mountain for the first time, or like finding a forest without roads or footpaths, or the blemish of an axe. You know then what you have always been told—that the world once lived and grew without adding machines and newsprint and brick-walled streets and the tyranny of clocks.—Beryl Markham

9:15 P.M., Talek River Camp

Again set up camp on the river. As we raise the tent, a leopard kills monkey in a tree a hundred yards away. Fire whipped by wind. Almost full moon. Peel potatoes and zucchini into bucket. Peels on ground might attract animals to the camp. Before going into tent, stare up through acacia lace at stars and the immensity of the universe of which I am such an infinitesimal part . . .

August 8, Saturday, 2:30 A.M.

Roaring lion awakens me from dream of a single white unicorn moving with migration. 153

As we drive toward Governor's Camp, five Cape buffalo stand facing us. With Elm Tree's approach they lunge off into tall reeds. What is it about them that is so fascinating? Their unpredictability? The sinister color of their hides and swing of their horns?

Topi

11:15 A.M. Ahead on plateau are mounds, perhaps three to four feet high and fifty yards apart. On each stands a topi, just as Rudolf Springer had described this place one hundred years ago. Behind plateau stretches grassland to trees, that snake along to indicate Mara River. Beyond trees and above them rises the Oloololo Escarpment.

It was Springer's belief that the topi act as sentinels for unicorns, to which they are distantly related. Indicates that topi, like some unicorns, have eyes light in color and whose black pupils give them look of intensity. Topi horns are more exotic and unusual then the single straight horn of the unicorn. This was the one animal that Springer learned lived in close association with *Unicornuus africanus.* "We found a plateau west of the river,"

he wrote, "upon which dozens of topi kept sentinel for the unicorn, warning them against intruders in a message that was communicated from one mound to another, carried across the lower lands to the river and up the escarpment by another flank of sentinels which stood guard on rocks at the very top of the Oloololo." Springer had also discovered this one of the few places, during his African observations, where birds engaged in mane-decorating activities that are so characteristic of unicorn-avian relationships in other parts of the world. However, he emphasized that not once did birds attempt to place flowers on topi sentinels.

3:30 P.M., bank of Mara River

After lunch, have fallen asleep on riverbank. A mosquito, fat-bodied, bulging with blood, has jabbed beak into skin on my knee. Is he of the chloroquine-resistant mutation, transmitting often fatal malaria to people in the East Africa I read about months ago in California? Tomorrow day for chloroquine. "Wip, wip, wee-ooo," the shrill notes of a red-chested cuckoo sound across the river.

6:21 P.M. Pitch tent few miles downriver at Crocodile Camp. Sit on grass as sun drops behind trees beyond which stretches plain and marsh. Lioness rests on a hill 400 yards away. Off to one side three bull Cape buffalo, one elephant, four impala, three warthogs, one waterbuck. Twenty feet from tent, below sixty-foot bank, twists the river where I see two Egyptian geese, four hippos, one very large crocodile. Fifty yards across, on the opposite bank, a group of five elephants emerges from the forest. Large cow tests air with trunk, then slowly walks down bank to drink as hippos blow in water left molten and glowing by sun dropping beyond escarpment.

How beautiful were the evenings of the Masai Reserve when after sunset we arrived at the river or the water-hole where we were to outspan, travelling . . . . The plains with the thorntrees on them were already quite dark, but the air was filled with clarity—and over our heads, to the West, a single star which was to grow big and radiant in the course of the night was now just visible, like a silver point in the sky of citrine topaz. The air was cold to the lungs, the long grass dripping wet, and the herbs on it gave out their spiced astringent scent. In a little while on all sides, the Cicada would begin to sing. The grass was me, and the air, the distant invisible mountains were me. . . . I breathed with the slight night-wind in the thorn-trees.—Karen Blixen

August 9, Sunday, 5:00 A.M., Crocodile Camp

Sleep is restless with anxiety dreams. Is it garlic I put in the macaroni and cheese or fear of not finding a unicorn?

6:55 *A.M.* Haddad ibis returns! A pair calling, "har, har, har, har," fly upriver. Luck with us? Burnt toast and rancid butter for breakfast.

10:06 A.M., Masai Mara

Stop to watch several thousand wildebeest thunder past, in single file, light flashing between their bodies as they wind off to form a large S against distant hillside.

8:30 P.M., Crocodile Camp

After dinner roast marshmallows. Lions roar, herons squawk from the river, hippos blow and growl, a hyena calls, baboons scream, crickets and night birds, wind plays tall grass and fire crackles.

There is something about safari life that makes you forget all your sorrows and feel the whole time as if you had drunk half a bottle of champagne,—bubbling over with heartfelt gratitude for being alive. It seems right that human beings should live in the nomad fashion and unnatural to have one's home always in the same place; one only feels really free when one can go in whatever direction one pleases over the plains, get to the river at sundown and pitch one's camp, with the knowledge that one can fall asleep beneath other trees, with another view before one, the next night. I had not sat by a camp fire for three years, and so sitting there again listening to the lions far out in the darkness was like returning to the really true world again,—where I probably once lived 10,000 years ago. . . . —Karen Blixen

10:00 *P.M.* Roars and splashes erupt the river. Walk to bank. In moonlight two hippos fight. Hopefully, they won't come here to graze on this night of full moon. Lightning flashes above the escarpment where I imagine a topi standing sentinel for white-as-the-moon single-horned animals that graze around him.

August 10, Monday, 4:00 A.M.

In half sleep heard a scream, then low rumbling. Heart skips beats as I fully awaken and hear low growling sound. Cup hands to ears and hold breath. Embarrassed. Realize that Bill's snoring has awakened me.

12:08 P.M., Elm Tree, Masai Mara

First male lion. Runs into grass before turning back, tail lashing, to stare at us. Springer writes of having seen adult lions and unicorns engaged in combined display ritual that he felt was responsible for their association in medieval crests and heraldry.

12:44 *P.M.* Lunch at Governor's Camp. Walk along riverbank searching for wildflowers to press into journal.

4:30 P.M., Crocodile Camp

From camp watch zebra stampede on the far side of marsh. Thundering across flat and up a hill, black-and-white stripes lost in dust. When dust settles, binoculars pick up lioness feeding on young zebra. Not easy to face reality that in several days, out of the reserve, will on foot have to approach totally wild lions. According to Springer, this must be done or attempts will later fail to approach unicorns. Across the marsh another lioness appears with two cubs. Leaves cubs at a tree a hundred yards away and walks over to start eating. African hoopoe in low voice calls from somewhere behind me, "hoo-hoo, hoo-hoo, hoo-hoo, ho, ho, ho!"

6:50 *P.M.* Sun has dropped. Lioness dozing in grass with cubs. Three Cape buffalo appear. Stop fifty yards away from cats, snort, horns held high. Lions raise heads. Largest bull starts advancing toward lions, then stops. Other bulls join him. Single lioness gets to feet, peers at buffalo, then dashes off into tall marsh grass. Buffalo begins walking toward lioness with cubs. Lioness backs off into dry grass, followed by cubs. Disappears. Buffalo continue to advance until arrive where lioness and cubs had been. Snort and toss heads, slicing air with black horns. There is no sign of the lioness and cubs. Finally, buffalo walk away.

August 11, Tuesday, 5:30 A.M.

"Hooee, hooee, hooee," the low whistle of an African scimitarb penetrates the tent. Imagine Springer exhausted after months of travel, almost certainly riddled with malaria and dysentery in that Africa of so long ago. He, however, was rewarded. And we haven't yet seen a white flash among the acacia trees or familiar heart-shaped footprint.

8:00 A.M., Elm Tree

Encounter lion pride. One male, four females, and one cub followed by larger male. One of the females carries a cub in her mouth for a short distance when the pride moves from formation of rock in the sun to shade of acacia trees. As I watch the large male slowly walk across the clearing, muscles flexing under the smoothness of his golden coat, I wonder if in several days I will have the courage to face a strange male lion on foot and allow it to approach within three inches of my body. George and Joy Adamson and Mark and Delia Owens had allowed the prides with whom they associated to slowly become accustomed to human beings. The Owenses had done their study in Botswana, an area where animals had had virtually no contact with humans and were neither frightened by nor felt aggression toward them. I will be using Rudolf Springer's Approach Formula in Kenya, where lions have long been in association with people and, with some frequency, eaten them. Perhaps in the hundred years since Springer utilized his four-step Approach Formula, animal behavior has changed to the extent that the body oil and other three steps for approach are no longer effective. Seeing the immenseness of the male lion before me—I worry.

12:00 P.M., Crocodile Camp

Hot. Lift jerrican rigged with a hose to be used for showers onto Elm Tree's luggage rack. Undress. Stand under cool water and soap myself. Suddenly feel am not alone. Being watched. Lion? Cape buffalo? Or an inoffensive bushbuck staring at me while I stand wet and naked? Then see it. Minibus has stopped a hundred yards away, barely visible through trees. Three gray-haired tourist ladies, heads protruding through the vehicle's roof hatches, are watching through binocular and cameras. With feet on the ground, I feel like one more animal in Masai Mara being scrutinized by tourists from Boston or Bristol or Barcelona. One more creature to provide them with stories to tell at lodge this evening. Stretch, bend over, and assume various poses, feeling that although most of the animals that women have observed during morning may have been placid, now they will see an active

one. Nearby, a ground hornbill voices a succession of deep, lionlike grunts.

August 12, Wednesday, 10:30 A.M., Elm Tree, foot of Ooololo Escarpment

We have reached base of the escarpment. Before starting the ascent, I review Springer's notes.

10:45 A.M. Climb is steep and made difficult by rocks overgrown with long, green grass that causes slippery footing. Every step must be carefully placed. Look back and can see and hear Mara River rushing over rocks.

11:00 A.M. Reaching upward to pull myself along, hand feels not only grass and stone, but something fragile, thin, and dry sends message from fingers to brain. Shed snakeskin. Cobra? Mamba? Adder?

11:45 A.M., top of Oloololo Escarpment

Reach ridge. No sign of life. Not even a solitary topi, only the "reum-ru-ra" song of an unidentifiable bird. Where are the dozens of antelope that Springer said once stood sentinel here? Where are the unicorns he studied? Where are the birds that engaged in the only mane-weaving activity that he was to observe in East Africa? "We haven't seen what you're looking for in four weeks," puffs Bill Wheeler out of breath from the climb. "We've talked to dozens of Masai, and not a single one has shown even the faintest glimmer of recollection when they've been shown your drawing. Forget it, Robert! You've found the Africa that you came looking for. Don't push your luck." He turns and starts down back toward Elm Tree.

12:00 P.M. Along the top of the Oloololo Escarpment, Joe and I hike through dry grass and low thorntrees. All we find is buffalo dung and part of a buffalo jawbone. Walk toward a higher point of the ridge. Slowly get whiff of fresh buffalo dung after which we cautiously move toward cluster of large boulders.

Climbing boulders, can see westward, the other side of escarpment, which is patchy savannah. Here little sign of even bird life. Then voices carried on the wind. The sound of cattle. Smoke in distance. So, like many other parts of the world, the Oloololo Escarpment has in a short hundred years been cleared of the wildlife that once prospered here, including unicorns. Replaced by men and cattle. Now only the Loita Hills, Nguruman Escarpment, and area between there and Ol Doinyo

Lengai remain to be explored. Will the remaining virgin forest in Kenya provide us last possibility to encounter *Unicornuus africanus*?

Africa is mystic; it is wild; it is a sweltering inferno; it is a photographer's paradise, a hunter's Vahalla, an escapist's Utopia. It is what you will, and it withstands all interpretations. It is the last vestige of a dead world or the cradle of a shiny new one. To a lot of people, as to myself, it is just "home." It is all these things but one thing—it is never dull.—Beryl Markham

1:05 P.M. As Joe and I start back to find more or less the place up which and now down which we will scale the escarpment, color catches my eye. A sudden flash of wings. Putting binoculars to eyes, a topi skull from which the bird has flown comes into focus. Rests on the top of a broken tree trunk. Who might have placed it there? Here certainly only a Masai. But why? Call Joe and we go to examine it. Skull is old. Worms have gotten to the horns. But strangest of all, it is decorated with delicate flowers. So topi and unicorn no longer roam the heights of the Oloololo Escarpment. A breed memory. The few birds that still reside here, desperate for something to decorate, have made use of the antelope skull. Unicorns were here! "Chaaaaaa, chaaaaaa," calls a rattling cisticola. Was it responsible for placement of flowers? Hands tremble as photograph skull and then start down face of the escarpment.

1:20 P.M. Stop to rest. Far below stretches Masai Mara, and the river. To the right a manyatta. (A manyatta is a village used for the initiation of warriors. The term *engang* is used to denote the village proper. However, during our safari the word *manyatta* seemed frequently to be used to describe any Masai settlement.) Just below is the Elm Tree. Now can see Bill talking to a group of Masai. Joe, with the binoculars to eyes, says, "Look, look at Bill!" Glancing back toward Land Rover, see Bill Wheeler waving hysterically and shouting to us, but distance and sound of the river makes words unintelligible.

1:55 P.M., Oloololo Escarpment

"I can't believe it! I'll never believe it!" screams Bill as he runs forward. "Robert, you were right! Robert, you were really right."

"About what?" I question, tired after the climb down. "About unicorns, Robert, you were right!" Bill's eyes blaze with excitement.

"You've seen my book. You've seen them there. But you're like a lot of other people who can't face up to beauty," I answer, ready to tell him that although unicorns today do not exist on the Oloololo Escarpment, they once did, and the decorated topi skull is proof of it. If he doesn't believe it, he can climb back up and see it for himself.

"No," he almost pleads. "I mean about unicorns in Africa! They are here—I don't mean right here, but where we're going."

"We've known that all along from Springer's journal," I answer, tired and aggravated.

"But that's something some guy could have invented. Look." He points to the Masai. "That guy was born in the Ngurumans, and he's seen a unicorn there with his own eyes."

I look toward four Masai, and the tall handsome one at whom Bill is gesturing. Masai approach. "Robert, this is Ben Kipeno." says Bill.

"Jambo," we greet each other and shake hands.

"My friend tells me that you know about animals that we are looking for. Where have you seen it?" I ask politely.

"Where you are going. Once you go to Keekorok, as your friend tells me, leave the gate of the park and you go to the forest and there you find this animal."

"To the Nguruman Forest?" questions Bill.

"No, it is not a government forest, it belongs to the Masai," answers Ben Kipeno, having misunderstood Wheeler's pronunciation. "It is a dense forest in the Loita Hills. There you will find some Masai, and they direct you into the bush."

What does this animal look like?" I ask.

"Like a zebra with a single horn on the top of its head," answers the Masai. "Just like the picture your friend has shown me."

Enthusiasm drops. The Masai may simply be describing the animal he has seen in the sketch, having never before even seen or heard of it—doesn't want to disappoint us by giving a negative answer to our question. However, there is a test that will prove if Ben Kipeno is telling the truth or not.

"Do you know what the animal is called? Do you know its name?" I ask.

"Its name is Nentikobe," answers the Masai with no hesitation.

Feel a rush of blood to face as look over at Bill. "It's true." Eyes moisten.

"Of course, it's true," smiles Bill. "But why didn't you tell us about this Nentikobe thing before? We could have asked the Masai we met in Olmoti or Embagai."

"Because if you had shown them the picture and given them the name, they might have said yes to any question you asked just to please you." (Since read "Nentikobe" in Springer's diary have never shared it with anyone.)

Turn back to Ben Kipeno. "And my friend tells me that you have seen the Nentikobe?"

"I have not seen it, but I have friends who have seen it. But you won't find them even if I tell you where they are. The forest is very dense where they live. And this won't take you there." He points to Elm Tree. "The place you want to visit is called Naimina Enkiyio."

"What does that mean?" asks Bill.

"It means the Forest of the Lost Children," answers Ben Kipeno.

"And what does 'Nentikobe' mean?" I ask,.

"It means the animal with one horn," answers Ben. "There are many strange animals that live in that forest."

"What are the others like?" asks Bill.

"They say there is one that has the appearance of a giant man with much hair. Like a gorilla, and it likes to fight men." Ben smiles to reveal the gap where one of his front teeth was removed in a Masai ceremony. "You see that whole place is a magic place. It is where the Laibons live."

"What are Laibons?" asks Bill.

"They are magicians, you know, traditional priests."

"And they live in the Forest of the Lost Children?" asks Bill.

"Some live there, but the most important ones live close to Ol Doinyo Lengai, which is a magical place. Some live in Naimina Enkiyio. You see, no trees have been cut there. It is very dense."

"Do the Masai go there often?" questions Joe.

"No, the forest is very dense," answers Ben.

"But are they afraid to go there?" asks Joe.

"Masai? No!" smiles Ben. "It is just that the forest is so thick."

"Do the Masai go to Ol Doinyo Lengai?" questions Bill, clearing his throat.

"Only the Laibons who do the rituals," answers Ben. "They bring back things from there for the whole tribe. Sometimes water. They come back and wash all the tribe with water. You go to a

Laibon, and he'll perform rituals. He takes cattle there, and when they come back they're more likely to increase in number. When women don't give birth, there is a permanent female magician at Ol Doinyo Lengai. She lives near a small crater there. She performs all the rituals there to give birth . . ."

"Is she a Laibon?" asks Bill.

"Not exactly," answers Ben Kipeno. "More or less a doctor. She helps give birth. She helps those with disease."

"Can the morani go there?" asks Bill.

"No, only the elders," answers Ben Kipeno.

"Are there any bad magicians, ones who don't do good magic?" asks Bill.

"Not really." Ben shifts legs assuming the Masai storklike stance. "Not around there. Though there are some."

"In the Forest of the Lost Children," I question, "have you ever heard of a very big tree near a waterfall?"

"That is a very special place," answers Ben.

"Why is it special?" I ask, remembering that not only Bill McGill mentioned this spot, but that Springer, in his diary, also wrote of a big tree near a waterfall in the forest at the edge of the Nguruman Escarpment where the Masai who accompanied him on his unicorn expeditions insisted on visiting. He reported that they did this to first cleanse their spears in a hot spring next to a large tree before continuing on to repeat the process in falls that were somewhere nearby. At the large tree also lived, at that time, the most powerful "witch doctor" in the area.

"The Masai who take you into the forest," continued Ben Kipeno, "will first have to go to that hot spring near the tree to wash their weapons in the water and then they must go to the falls and do the same thing. If they do not do this, you will not see Nentikobe."

"What color is Nentikobe?" I ask.

"They say it is like shiny metal. You know, like silver," answers Ben Kipeno.

"You mean white?" questions Joe.

"They say it is very bright like silver," responds Ben, again shifting his leg positions, resting the arch of his left foot against the calf of his right leg.

"He means bright white," says Bill softly at my shoulder.

I smile and look at Dr. Wheeler. "A half hour ago you couldn't have cared less about unicorns, and now you're putting words in this man's mouth to try and convince yourself they exist."

"Don't be silly," says Bill seriously. "Of course, white in the right light can look silver. Haven't you ever seen a white horse in the sun after it's bathed?"

We thank Ben Kipeno for his information, exchange addresses, shake hands, and say, *"Kwaheri."* Just as Bill is putting Elm Tree into first gear, Ben sticks his head through the window. "Look, when you go to Entaskera, you ask for Rafael. He is a Masai who speaks English. He was a sergeant major in the army. He is a good man. He once worked as a tracker for safaris. He will help you."

Elm Tree lurches forward. Bill clears his throat. "Well, I guess that's it. Robert, I never believed it, but there is a unicorn. That man has seen it."

"Bill," I say, "that man did not see a unicorn. He knows people who saw it who told him about their experience. There's a difference between actually having seen one and being told about someone having seen one."

2:45 P.M., Elm Tree, road to Masai Serena Lodge

As Elm Tree rattles along, ponder Ben Kipeno's story. Although Peter Matthiessen had never mentioned the Nentikobe, he had written about the forest giant described by Ben:

From where I watched, a sentinel in the still summer, there rose and fell the night highlands of two countries, from the Loita down the length of the Ngurumans to the Sonjo scarps that overlook Lake Natron. In the Loita, so the Maasai say, lives Enenauner, a hairy giant, one side flesh, the other stone, who devours mortal men lost in the forests; Enenauner carries a great club, and is heard tokking on trees as it moves along. A far hyena summoned the night feeders, and flamingos in crescents moved north across a crescent moon toward Naivasha and Nakuru. Down out of the heavens came their calls, a remote electric sound, as if in this place, in such immensities of silence, one had heard heat lightning.

3:10 P.M., Elm Tree, road to Keekorok

Stop at Masai Serena Lodge for lunch. Tame hyrax sits in sun on stone wall at lodge entrance. Our aspect makes me feel as though we are fugitives from a Humphrey Bogart film. Dirty and unshaven walk through dining room of manicured, clean tourists. Bill can't stop talking about unicorns. From dining terrace of lodge, next to the swimming pool, splendid view of the plain, beyond which is Mara River. Tourists can eat here and at the same time watch the animals grazing below. "Now when it comes right down to it," I say to Joe and Bill as we sit down, "not that many people really care about the animals."

"They should use the Golden Rule with them as well as people," says Joe. "I mean do unto others as you would have them do unto you. With animals being the 'others.'"

"The Golden Rule is being used," I answer. "And someday those zebra and giraffe grazing down there will be as rare and hard to find on earth as is the Nentikobe."

"What do you mean?" asks Joe. "If they used the Golden Rule they'd be thinking of the animals."

"The Golden Rule they use isn't yours." I watch a zebra foal running, bucking, and leaping around its mother. "The land developers' Golden Rule reads that gold rules."

"Yeah." Bill comes to life under his pith helmet. "You can't stop money. It can be done, but it's hard to win a fight with a man who's richer than you. There's more money in oil and timber and cattle than there is in conservation. One day giraffe and elephant and hippopotamus will live only in men's imaginations and on the printed pages of books. They'll be creatures of mythology and fantasy, so rare that their existence will be doubted as the unicorn's is today."

4:22 P.M., Elm Tree, road to Keekorok

Elm Tree bounces forward as I lament having missed seeing wildebeest cross the river. Suddenly, Joe says, "What is that smoke there?"

"Where?" Bill asks.

"Over there by the river," Joe motions to the left.

Wheeler lifts pith helmet higher on his brow, squinting eyes more than usual. Eyes start to blink rapidly.

"Watch the road!" I shout as Elm Tree, out of control, begins to cut across open country.

"It's dust!" screams Bill. "That's not smoke. It's got to be a river crossing. I can't believe this. Those Japanese television guys waited two years. I waited two weeks, and here on our last day in Masai Mara, there's a river crossing!"

Bill turns Elm Tree off the road. Roar full barrel

migration crossing at Mara River, August 11

across open country, with the cloud of dust and river probably a mile away.

4:30 P.M., Elm Tree, Mara River

Stop on outcrop looking over the river. A quarter mile away, crossing surges forward. Bill sets up tripod and movie camera. Joe and I stand stunned by the scene that is taking place in the distance. Put 300-millimeter lens on camera and look through viewfinder. Crossing too far away for still cameras, but close enough for the lens on Bill's movie camera.

"Come on!" I shout to Bill. "We can't photograph it from here. It's too far away."

"But I'm all set up," he shouts back.

"But you've seen it before. Joe and I never have. We have to get closer." Photographer's instinct put into panic by knowing that second by second losing marvelous material. See Bill has no intention of moving, "Come on, Bill!" I shout angrily. "It's not fair. You've seen it before. Please drive us down there."

"You take the Land Rover!" he shouts back, not removing his eye from Bolex viewfinder.

"There's no time," I realize, "even with the Land Rover." More than half of the animals have crossed. "I'm going, Joe," I shout and grab camera bag.

Bill pulls his head back from camera. "You can't go anywhere. It's crazy. Take the Land Rover."

"There isn't time to try and find a way over there. Are you coming?" Joe has picked up his camera bag.

"You can't. Robert, don't be stupid. At one of these crossings there are always lions along the bank waiting for the wildebeest. Look at those buffalo trails down to the water. You can't run over there!"

"I'm going!" I sling bag over shoulder and start to run. Bank is uneven, and lined with brush, cut by animal trails leading down to water. Sprinting all out, second camera banging against my chest, right hand steadying bag and left hand on big telephoto lens of first camera. Joe dashing along beside me.

Foolishly, for certain, don't think of lion, elephant, rhino, leopard, or Cape buffalo, only the crossing that is going on ahead and that my camera is missing it.

Stop one hundred yards from the crossing. In water and on far bank, antelope and zebra still crashing into one another and surging through foam and dust. Higher on bank, wildebeest thrust selves into air, crash into river, disappearing beneath surface. Cameras fire.

Then last of the herd, shiny wet black, trudging out of water into cloud of dust left behind by thousands of animals, moving toward Serengeti Plain. Hundred yards upriver, four hippos blow and face in our direction. Across the water five giraffe calmly graze among thorntrees. "Gaarr, waarr," calls a white-bellied go-away bird.

6:15 P.M., Elm Tree, road to Keekorok

To right, only a mile away, is the Tanzania border and the beginning of the Serengeti. Just beyond somewhere in the same direction, the Sand River.

8:30 P.M., Keekorok Lodge

Simon Ole Makallah, chief warden of Masai Mara, accepts our dinner invitation. Delightful man, compassionate, intelligent with a marvelous sense of humor. Talk of American parks and their problems, of allowing too many people into reserves at one time, and of permitting people to get out of cars in game areas.

As evening wears on, feel an affinity with fine man sitting across the table, and finally ask, "Simon, have you ever seen Nentikobe?"

Simon Makallah smiles, revealing not only a flash of white but the place where also one of his teeth had been extracted in Masai ceremony. "Who told you about that?" he questions. "I've never ever had a white man ask me about that."

"I've known about it for some time," I answer. "That's why in part that I'm here. To find it."

"But it doesn't exist." His smile is wider. "It is a creature of legend."

"What do you know about it?" I ask.

"It is an invention to keep children out of the deep forest. People tell them that if they go into the forest, the Nentikobe will catch them. (Simon Makallah used the Masai word *Nentiboke* as contrasted to Springer's *Nentikobe*.) They say it uses its front legs to kill you. That you cannot run away from it. No, I don't believe you have come here looking for Nentikobe."

"I've seen it," I say, looking deep into Simon Makallah's eyes. "Where is it supposed to be found?"

"Well," he answers, "if that is what you are looking for, you are going to exactly the right place—the Forest of the Lost Children. Come to my office in the morning," he smiles, "and we will talk more about it."

August 13, Thursday, 3:30 A.M., camp, Keekorok

Brought awake by low rumbling. Raise head slightly and stare into Joe's wide-open eyes. Something smacks part of tent touching my hip. Lion's tail swats it again as rumbling growl accelerates. From hours spent with lions doing cat book, know this vocalization is one of the most aggressive and dangerous sounds that a lion uses, generally issued just before attack. Lion is so close can hear its stomach gurgling. Then it starts! Two lions fighting just beside the tent. Even Bill Wheeler, who sleeps through anything, is awakened. Cats lunging, screaming, and running all around tent. Finally, the battle moves away. Then silence, except for the soft cry of an African scops owl.

Put head back on the khaki rolled-up jacket that serves as a pillow. Heart pounding. With fear? Battle was so near, sounds so intense. Finally, Joe whispers, "Boy, that was close." Now I can think only of what I must do within the next week if, by Springer's formula, we are able to approach a unicorn—first approach elephant as close as three inches, and then lion. The same questions swirl my mind. What if time has made the Springer formula ineffective? What if it simply doesn't work anymore? Like distant vulture, worry circles mind, which finally lands in sleep.

10:00 A.M. office of Warden Simon Makallah, Keekorok

"Do you know Ben Kipeno?" I ask.

"Oh, you met him. Yes, he is a good man," answers Simon.

"He told us that when we arrived at Entaskera, we should look for a man called Rafael who will help us organize the foot safari into the Loita Hills, that is, the Forest of the Lost Children, to the Nguruman Escarpment, down to Lake Natron, and as far as we can get toward Ol Doinyo Lengai."

"Yes, Rafael is the right person. He is a good man. But tell me, is it really the Nentikobe that you are looking for?"

"Why not?" I smile.

"Because, as I told you last night," says Simon Makallah patiently, "that is only a legend. This animal does not exist. It is a story that people use to frighten the children from going into the forest where they can become lost or lose the cattle they are herding. I have been there many times, you know. In fact, I am trying to have it made into a national park. Several of the boys who are working for me here are from that area. Here, let me call some of them." He rises from the table, goes to the door, and speaks to a secretary.

While we are waiting for the men to appear, Simon tells about the Masai high school that he has helped to build and how desperate they are for texts in English. We promise that upon returning home, we will try to find discarded schoolbooks to send him. Knock at door. Dressed in park ranger uniform, a handsome Masai youth enters room. "This is Shadrack Ole Lensir," Simon makes introduction. Shake hands. "I was telling Dr. Wheeler and his friends," continues Simon, "that you are from the Loita Hills. They are going to Entaskera to form a foot safari to the falls and down to Lake Natron. Ben Kipeno gave them the name of Rafael."

Simon Ole Makallah

"Yes, Rafael is good," replies Shadrack, respectfully.

"Do you want to ask Shadrack anything?" Simon looks at me.

Stare into boy's seemingly innocent eyes. "Yes, have you ever heard of Nentikobe?" I question.

"I have seen him," the boy replies seriously.

"You have what?" Simon bursts with laughter.

"I have seen the Nentikobe." The boy smiles nervously.

"What does it look like?" asks Bill Wheeler, clearing his throat as eyelids flutter nervously.

"Well, it appears like a zebra with one horn on its head. Right in the center." He touches his forehead. "And its color is very bright. You know, like silver."

"Have you seen it more than once?" I question excitedly.

"Yes, several times," answers Shadrack. "But it is not easy to see. You see, it stays only in the very deep forest."

"Ho-ha-ha," Simon's ample body rocks with laughter. "You say, Shadrack, that you have seen that thing? Not once but twice?"

Shadrack grins anxiously. "Yes, I have. I really have, and other people have seen him also."

A second ranger comes into room and Simon addresses him, "What do you think, Shadrack says he has seen the Nentikobe, one of our own

rangers? And these men," he gestures to us, "are going into the Loita Hills to look for it."

"Well," laughs the newcomer, "if you find Nentikobe and bring him back here, I will give you one cow. And, you know, to a Masai cattle are very important."

"And I," says Simon "will give you ten wildebeest and a case of beer."

We all laugh, though Shadrack's is obviously forced and self-conscious. "Can you show us on a map where you saw this animal?" I ask him.

We say good-bye to Warden Makallah, and Shadrack accompanies us to Elm Tree. Bill grabs map from front seat, spreads it on Land Rover hood, and with his finger traces our route into the Loita Hills and forward to Entaskera. Shadrack volunteers names of relatives, and as we say good-bye, he asks, "Do you know about the Masai having to go to the water at the tree of the Laibons and then to the waterfall to clean the blood from their spears before they will accompany you?"

"We know," I reply.

"Then you may see Nentikobe." He smiles.

"Thank you, Shadrack." I shake his hand, and as if to reassure myself, ask one last time, "You really did see the Nentikobe?"

The smile leaves the Masai boy's face. "You have my word I have seen the Nentikobe, the first time was at four o'clock in the afternoon, and he does exist and lives where you are going even though others do not believe this. It is just that they have not seen him, and unless you have seen something with your own eyes, how can you believe that it lives?"

2:51 P.M., Elm Tree, main road to Narok and Nairobi

Leave main highway and turn off on the dirt road that will take us to Entaskera. Now feel that we have left everything superficial about this trip behind. Ahead there are no white-faced people speaking German, Japanese, English, or Dutch. No laws to keep us from getting out of Elm Tree.

Ahead of me lies a land that is unknown to the rest of the world and only vaguely known to the African—a strange mixture of grasslands, scrub, desert sand like long waves of the southern ocean. Forest, still water, and age-old mountains, stark and grim like mountains of the moon. Salt lakes, and rivers that have no water. Swamps. Badlands. Land without life. Land teeming with life—all of the dusty past, all of the future.—Beryl Markham

3:30 P.M., Elm Tree, Loita Hills

Five ground hornbills. Game starts to appear as move farther from blacktop road and civilization. Sky has clouded and first rain drops fall. Directly ahead, for miles, road stretching off golden into the distance to the purple mountains that stand dark and ominous in the distance. Two dik-dik, flock of guineas scatter.

4:26 P.M., Elm Tree, Nauroshura, Loita Hills

As we leave village of Nauroshura, in late afternoon, cross a stream above which yellow fever trees spread, in delicate patterns before cloud-shadowed mountains. Earth changes in color from gray and tan to deep red-orange. A lone wildebeest. And far, far off in the distance, two red-draped Masai.

The Natives were Africa in flesh and blood. The tall extinct volcano of Longonot that rises above the Rift Valley, the broad Mimosa trees along the rivers, the Elephant and the Giraffe, were not more truly Africa than the Natives were,—small figures in an immense scenery. All were different expressions of one idea, variations upon the same theme. It was not a congenial upheaping of heterogeneous atoms, but a heterogeneous unheaping of congenial atoms, as in the case of the oak-leaf and the acorn and the object made from oak. We ourselves, in boots, and in our constant great hurry, often jar with the landscape. The Natives are in accordance with it, and when the tall, slim, dark, and dark-eyed people travel—always one by one, so that even, the great Native veins of traffic are narrow foot-paths,—or work the soil, or herd their cattle, or hold their big dances, or tell you a tale, it is Africa wandering, dancing and entertaining you. —Karen Blixen

5:10 P.M., Elm Tree, Loita Hills

Now at the foot of the mountains. Bill stops Elm Tree and we climb out into the coolness. Red earth is still wet from recent rain. Dampness refreshing. Zebra feeds in a clearing of Gauguin colors a hundred yards away.

"Let's camp here," I suggest to Bill and Joe. "Now that we're where we want to be, we should wind down. If this is going to be a success, from now on it has to be well planned, following Springer's instructions."

5:23 P.M. Bill drives Elm Tree off road, guided by open spaces among the trees, to a secluded spot under far-reaching acacias. Tent is raised.

Camping places fix themselves in your mind as if you had spent long periods of your life in them. You will remember a curve of your waggon track in the grass of the plain, like the features of a friend.—Karen Blixen

7:45 P.M., camp, Loita Hills

Finish dinner of canned beans and spaghetti. After Bill and Joe have done dishes, sit around campfire. Prolonged "tok-tok-tok-tok" of Mozambique nightjar. Silence except for night sounds until Bill clears throat and asks, "Well. What do we have to do? Robert, what's the plan?"

"We're going to follow Springer to the letter," I reply. "Today is the thirteenth of August, Thursday. That means between now and the thirty-first, when we leave Nairobi, we have only a little more than two weeks. We've been here, that is, I've been here, thirteen days. Springer's journal says that before a person can use the Approach Formula and apply the body oil, he has to be in Africa ten days. And before the formula is used with unicorns, it has to be tried on elephant and lion." I throw a log on the fire and go to the Land Rover.

"What are you doing?" asks Bill.

"Just a minute," I reply as I feel my way through a blue canvas carryon bag until contact is made with the small, cool, bottle. Back at the fire I begin to take off my clothes.

"What are you doing?" questions Bill.

Shirt, pants, socks, and underwear draped over camp chair, stand on boots so that the oil I have begun to apply to my feet will not pick up dirt. "This is the third step in Springer's plan. I cover my body with this oil."

"Boy, it stinks," says Joe with a grimace. "A baboon smells sweet compared to that."

The oil uncomfortably spread to every part of my body, I stand glistening before the flames, allowing skin a chance to absorb it.

"Do we have to do that, too?" Bill asks apprehensively.

A hyena whoops in the distance. "No, only me," I reply. "If this doesn't work for any reason, I'm not going to be responsible for getting you killed."

"Then we're not going to get close to elephants, lions, or see unicorns?" Bill asks seriously. "Only you?"

"You're going to get closer to elephants and lions than most people, close enough to photograph me with them, but not close enough to get yourselves killed. And, if this works and they really are still in these forests, you will see a unicorn."

"Well, what about the rest of that Approach Formula? What else do you have to do?"

"Apart from the oil, I've already taken two of the other steps, and the fourth I'll do when we're with the animals."

"But can't you tell us what they are?" questions Bill. "What if something happens to you? Then Joe or I'd have to try it."

"Bill," I say, starting to put on my clothes, "if something happens to me, then it would be crazy for either of you to try. Anyway, I feel that if the Springer material has been in some way entrusted to me, it has to stay with me."

"How long do you have to leave that stuff on?" Bill wrinkles up his nose as I pass him on way to return bottle of oil to Land Rover.

"Until we've finished our work, I can't take it off," I reply.

"And you're going to sleep in the same tent with us for two weeks with that stuff on?" he asks.

The hyena whoops closer now. "You want to see unicorns?" I ask. There is no reply but crackling of the fire, night insects, and, again, the hyena.

August 14, Friday, 2:10 A.M.

Awaken to the distant roar-wheeze of lion. Look at my watch. In the darkness can see Bill is awake, looking at me. "You awake?"

"How could anyone sleep with that stink? It's giving me a headache," he complains. "I'm not surprised you're going to get that close to lions with that stuff on. What would eat anything that smelled like you? I was thinking, weren't we first going to see that Masai, Rafael, to start the foot safari into the Forest of the Lost Children, and then to the hot springs and falls?"

"We can't," I whisper, trying not to wake Joe, who is sleeping between us. "Springer says that the formula won't work with elephants and lions if Masai are taken along and only with unicorns after the spears have been washed in hot springs and falls. We'll spend the next four or five days looking for elephant and lion to try this out, then we'll go on to Entaskera. We have only two weeks. If we don't follow Springer's instructions exactly, the whole thing could be ruined."

"Okay," he says softly and puts his head back on his rolled-up jacket. I do the same and hope for sleep, thinking that in a few hours I may be face to face, three inches away from a wild, adult, African elephant.

11:35 A.M., Elm Tree, Loita Hills

Have spent all morning scouting for elephant. Even freshest signs appear weeks old. Remind ourselves that we are out of the reserve and no longer dealing with animals in a tourist park. While Bill and Joe walk slowly ahead, I stop to gather and press wildflowers.

2:05 P.M. Have searched and driven for hours. So discouraged that the occasional antelope or zebra, which would have found its way onto these pages, is barely seen and not noted. Elephant is what we are after.

2:38 P.M. Have left Elm Tree and are making a quarter-mile circle when suddenly there is the sound of large animals ahead. Climb ridge. Pool fed by muddy stream is full of hippopotami. Maybe fifty of them. Downwind, and asleep in the warm sun, they do not detect our presence. Tell Bill and Joe that with only a few good hours of light left in day, we will study hippos. As I sit taking notes, think of Odell Shepard: "Compared to the unicorn, the hippopotamus is a nightmare, the giraffe highly improbable." *Charaxes candiope* butterflies cluster at water's edge.

4:05 P.M., Loita Hills

Elm Tree's climb up into mountains is slow. Now in true forest. Vegetation lush and thick along sides of red-earthed road, partly washed out by recent rain. Lion's tail and black-eyed Susans fleck orange the green passageway through hills.

5:45 P.M. Darkness approaching. For the past hour we have been driving through the highlands. Setting pastoral, except where the forest walls up around meadows and clearings. But for a few Masai children herding cattle and an occasional antelope, little sign of life. Then road forks, larger path to right, smaller one with grass growing in its center, to left. From map would appear smaller road leads to Entaskera, which now must be very near. Continuing with plan, we go right, which will hopefully lead us down out of the maintains and to elephant.

6:00 P.M. Two Masai appear ahead on right side of the road. Stop. "Jambo." Shake hands and ask for Entaskera. With a toothless smile, one of men motions back in the direction from which we have just come, and indicates that somewhere we should have turned to left. Speak rapidly. Repeats in English the word *back.*

9:00 P.M., Edge of Nguruman Escarpment

Journey out of the hills in the darkness is slow going and twisty. At last we reach foothills at edge of plain, drive a mile off the dirt road, and make camp. So tired, we eat only beef jerky and Bill's week-old bread.

August 15, Saturday, 2:15 A.M., Elephant Camp

While lion repeats wheeze at end of roar, somewhere off along escarpment elephant trumpets. They are here. The oil that was so rank-smelling the day before now does not bother my nostrils when nose touches shoulder. Lion has finished call, and before I drop off to sleep no further sound comes from the elephant. Think of other animal studies. Ian Douglas-Hamilton, author of *Life Among the Elephants,* became so familiar with the animals he watched that he could literally make physical contact with them, as had Jane Goodall with chimpanzees, Dian Fossey with gorillas, and Mark and Delia Owens with brown hyenas. But those naturalists had spent long hours with their subjects before a bond of mutual confidence was established. In the next few days I will have to sit and wait to be approached by wild creatures who may at one time have been hunted by man, whom they either fear or despise.

6:30 A.M., Elm Tree, edge of Nguruman Escarpment

Animals begin to take form in new light. Some stare at Elm Tree, others dash away or alongside. Two giraffe appear, turn, and cross in a pas de deux. Remember Karen Blixen's words: "Giraffe, in their . . . inimitable, vegetative gracefulness . . . rare, long-stemmed, speckled, gigantic flowers slowly advancing."

10:10 A.M. After searching for hours, suddenly three boulderlike shapes move through the thorn-trees ahead—cow elephants, two with tusks, one without. Nearest faces us, from two hundred yards, raises trunk, fans her ears, then all three turn and fast walk to lose themselves in trees.

10:32 A.M. Each time we approach, cows move away. "That formula isn't working," Bill finally says. "I've gotten closer to elephants before—without you or it."

Not discouraged, but puzzled, wonder why formula is not effective. Doing something wrong. Confidence in Springer is total. "Look," I say to Bill and Joe. "let's see if we can find another group of elephants. When we do, you stay back and let me go ahead. You're not using the formula, that may be the trouble. You stay behind and put on your big telephoto lenses, and let's see what happens."

"Yeah, if we can find more elephants," Bill says solemnly.

11:05 A.M. Bull elephant standing in acacia trees three hundred yards away. Back toward us. Pick up dust and let it fall to air—we are downwind.

11:09 A.M. Have crept to within one hundred yards of elephant, who continues dozing. "You stay here," I say to Bill and Joe, "and have your cameras ready. One way or another, you'll get good pictures."

11:13 A.M. Now, emerging into a clearing that separates us, am within fifty yards of the elephant. Certainly he must be able to hear heart smash-pounding in my chest, booming in my ears. Rise up from brush and take ten steps toward tusker, using vocalizations for elephant approach as indicated by Springer. Can see elephant's sides heaving. Stands off to my right. Vocalize again. He slowly turns. Ears fan out. Make eye contact. Use the fifth of Springer's prescribed vocalizations. Continues to stare at me. Cup hands around my mouth and make final of Springer's instructed sounds. The only answer is the purring "pip, ir, ee," of a white-browed robin chat.

11:15 A.M. Tusker watches for almost two minutes, raises trunk, trumpets three times, and then slowly starts to walk to left. Three blasts indicate, if Springer is correct, that I have been accepted. Turn around, smile at Bill and Joe, both of whom, fifty yards away, have faces pressed tightly to cameras. Suddenly, Bill drops camera and screams, "Robert, he's charging." Bull elephants, like stag unicorns, often engage in mock charges. Springer was frequently confronted with this seemingly dangerous situation, in which the observer, if he has been anointed with the twenty-six ingredient oil, must merely stand his ground. Confidence is such that, holding my camera, I remain facing Bill and Joe, both of whom have dropped cameras and have terrified expressions on faces.

Can hear pounding of the bull elephant's feet. "Take pictures," I shout to my companions, both frozen in terror. Then there is a swirl of dust as the tusker stops beside me. Trunk touches my shoulder as it extends, testing the air for their scent. Feel his white tusks brush my white legs. Seems not as aware of my presence—as though I were an antelope or zebra or other wild creature with which he is familiar. Slowly turn and look up at the immensity of the creature that is standing less than a foot away.

Then swing around to see Bill and Joe, white-faced, staring, as if frozen to the spot. "Take some pictures," I shout at them, at which sound the bull elephant takes several steps forward, then turns slowly around, crosses the clearing, and disappears into trees.

When I reach Bill and Joe, they both seem in shock. "Why didn't you keep taking pictures?" I ask. "If we don't have another elephant encounter, no one will believe it."

Finally, Bill speaks, blinking nervously, "Robert, take pictures! I thought he was going to mow you down. I've never seen anything like that. I can't believe I've seen what I've just seen! You did see it, Joe?"

Joe smiles. "I saw it. Remember, I've also seen unicorns with Robert. I was just startled. Though, I did get a picture just as he started to charge with your back toward him.

"I still can't believe it," exclaims Bill. "No one will."

2:30 P.M., Elm Tree, edge of Nguruman Escarpment

Fresh signs of elephant everywhere, yet we haven't seen another one since the bull with whom I made contact. Black shapes loom at the edge of the forest, wading through shadows of yellow fever trees. A herd of buffalo. "Try it with them," urges Bill, stopping the Land Rover.

"Springer said they're the only member of the big five with which the formula won't work. He tried it several times and almost lost his life doing so." The heads of the buffalo are up. Staring back at them, I recall a magazine story that Beryl Markham wrote:

I see not one but a dozen buffalo heads emerging from the bush, across our path like links in an indestructible chain . . . I knew what African buffaloes were. I knew it was less dangerous to come upon a family of lions in the open plain than to come upon a herd of buffaloes, or to come upon a single buffalo; everyone knew it—everyone except amateur hunters who liked to roll the word "lion" on their lips. Few lions will attack a man unless they are goaded into it; most buffaloes will. A lion's charge is swift and often fatal, but if it is not, he bears no grudge. He will not stalk you but a buffalo will. A buffalo is capable of mean cunning that will match the mean cunning of the men who hunt him, and every time he kills a man he atones for the death at men's hands of many of his species. He will gore you, and when you are down he will kneel upon you and grind you into the earth.

Drive on in search of elephant.

2:45 P.M. "We're wasting time," says Bill, as he stops Elm Tree, removes straw pith helmet, and wipes sweat from his forehead. "We've got to get pictures of you with the elephants or nobody really will believe this."

"Springer's formula," I reply, "calls for two elephant and two lion encounters before trying it with a unicorn. We've already used up one elephant encounter. With the next one, if we can find them, I'd like to do a herd, with at least three or four adults."

"Why aren't you taking notes on all the other animals we see?" asks Joe inquisitively. "When we started the trip, you were looking at your pad most of the time, noting every zebra, every ostrich."

"It's like the photographer when he first visits Africa," I smile. "You take pictures of everything, all the common animals, and as time goes by and you see there are so many, you begin to focus on the really difficult and interesting ones."

"That's what I did," says Bill. "You should see all the awful stuff I took of zebra, wildebeest, and gazelle. But then you learn. Anyhow, the only thing I want to do now is get something with the elephants and you."

3:00 P.M. We drive closer to the edge of escarpment, where the forest begins. Park Elm Tree. Start walking.

3:15 P.M. Sounds of elephant through trees. Take cover behind a termite mound and slowly peer around it. Seventy yards away four dark

august 15, edge of Ngurumen Escarpment

shapes among the green: one old cow, two young bulls, and a calf. "Let's try for them," whispers Bill. "Go ahead," he motions me forward with his head.

"It's not what I want," I whisper back. "We need three or four adult animals. Anyway, the vegetation is too dense in here for you to get anything good. Let's go back to the edge of the plain where it's more open."

3:16 P.M. "Stop!" shouts Joe. "Look over there!" He points right, toward the open plain. Swinging the binoculars slowly along, a startling, large gray shape fills them. A bull elephant!

"Look at that!" I hand Bill the field glasses.

"Man, I've never seen ivory like that. Look at that! Those tusks! Now we've got to get a picture of you right between them." He puts Elm Tree into gear and starts toward the gray mass on the horizon.

A quarter of a mile from the elephant, we stop once more. "How are we going to do this?" asks Joe.

"We're not going to do it," I reply.

"You? Afraid?" Bill clears his throat.

"A little bit," I answer, "but that's not the reason. Are you sure you got at least a couple of frames of me with that other bull?" I ask Joe.

"For sure I got him when he started walking along behind you, and then when he swung around, flared his ears, and charged. I got that. But then I stopped when he kept coming."

"That's all we need with a single animal." I study the bull with the field glasses. "Between now and tomorrow we have to find a herd. Tomorrow's the sixteenth. On the seventeenth we have to start after lion." Looking at the elephant, alone in the world, plains stretching out around him and the seemingly never-ending sky overhead, while his wonderful ivory moves from side to side through the grass. I recall, "the shark is hunted for its fin, the elephant for its tusks, and the rhino for its horn—then what price the unicorn?"

9:00 P.M., camp, edge of Nguruman Escarpment
After dinner (tuna, macaroni and cheese, and the last of Brussels sprouts turning to mold in a basket in the back of Elm Tree) when the dishes have been done, we sit around the campfire. Bill and Joe seem unusually silent.

"Is everything alright?" Look across the fire at them.

"Well, it's just that what if we don't find elephant tomorrow?" says Bill. "We still have to find

lion and then go back to Entaskera and organize the foot safari. Walk through the Forest of the Lost Children to the falls, and then to the escarpment and down toward Lake Natron and Ol Doinyo Lengai. That's a lot to do, and we haven't yet seen a unicorn."

"Tomorrow we'll find elephant," I answer. "Be positive. Think, so far everything's gone well. We've tried the formula and it works. Tomorrow we'll find them."

August 16, Sunday, 2:15 A.M., tent, edge of Nguruman Escarpment
Waken to the sounds of African night that no longer cause anxiousness or fear, but lull me back to sleep.

12:30 P.M., edge of Nguruman Escarpment
No luck. We have driven back and forth along the escarpment. See only giraffe, zebra, wildebeest, warthog, and ostrich.

1:25 P.M. After peanut butter and jelly sandwich, leave Elm Tree and start out on foot. Going is slow, not because of the terrain, but because the sense of danger is strong in heavy vegetation. Elephant, lion, rhino, and leopard pose a threat to Joe and Bill, who are not wearing the oil—and Cape buffalo to all of us.

2:15 P.M., edge of Nguruman Escarpment
Hear it! Cup hands out behind ears to amplify sound. Elephant, somewhere ahead. Maybe a half mile away. Joe picks up dry grass. Drops it. Wind with us.

3:03 P.M. Have come so slowly, knowing that the slightest mistake will send the elephants silently off into vegetation, possibly not to be seen again today.

Pair of lilac-breasted rollers soar, then return to high, dead branches of a tree at far end of clearing. Under acacias, we count one, two, three, four, five, six adult elephants. Largest two are tuskless. Remember reading Bror Blixen—"tuskless elephants are the most dangerous of all." Wind is still with us.

"I'm going to that fallen tree. See it?" I ask Bill and Joe. "Almost covered in grass directly in front of us, twenty feet from the elephant herd. Once I get there and sit down, I'm going to try and imitate a call that Springer describes to bring them out from under the trees and to me. If this works, you come as carefully through the grass as possible until you're close enough to take pictures."

3:09 P.M. Now in the middle of the clearing and raise up from the bent-over position that has kept me hidden in grass. Use the first of the four vocalizations, according to Springer's instruction. Elephants immediately turn around, fan out ears, raise trunks, searching the wind, which has now changed and is carrying Bill's and Joe's scent to them. Begin walking toward them at same time, voice second call prescribed by Springer. Larger cow, with white stumps for tusks, turns slightly, but continues browsing. Others still face in this direction. I move very slowly.

3:11 P.M. Arrive at dead tree and sit down. Remove pen and note pad. Begin making notes on elephants' behavior. Now all have resumed feeding.

3:20 P.M. Turn toward elephants ripping and snapping limbs off thorntrees. Wonder, even with tough hides, how they can smash among thorns and not be hurt. Now, before they move off, time to call them up to me. Have marveled at my brother calling ducks in the Imperial Valley. Of watching specks in the sky, flying southward when Ron would start "quack-quack" to bring them spiraling down to the water in front of us. Remember another friend who, by imitating call of dying rabbit, could summon coyotes to within a few feet of us. Jim Corbett could, in India, bring tiger and leopard right up to him by imitating the mating yawl or the sound of another male cat.

Put hands to mouth, bring air up from lungs, and use the slow vocalization that Springer spelled out actually by musical notes in his journal. Large cow with broken-off tusks responds immediately and starts out of trees toward me. Sound call again and other elephants follow. Indian elephants I have stood among and ridden, but not even that was preparation for the immensity of the African ones that are now coming forward through the grass.

Glance toward Bill and Joe, but cannot see them. Elephants fifty feet away. Twenty. Ten. Five. Here! Difficult to be casual, but try. Feel sweat spreading out under arms. Will it wash away oil and will my own smell agitate elphants now towering next to me? Try to keep from making eye contact. Feel air moved by flapping of their ears. Suddenly, a trunk brushes across my shoulder, then against my cheek. Anxiety subsides. Glance forward and see wake in tall grass indicating that Bill and Joe are approaching.

3:35 P.M. When Joe and Bill raise up from grass sixty yards away, fear they may frighten elephants, who take no notice and stand swaying or dozing around me. One of younger cows begins throwing dirt onto her back. As in equine study in the Camargue, for the book *Such is the Real Nature of Horses*, make no physical contact with the animals I am observing. Allow them to touch me, but don't put hands on them. To have stood next to the bull elephant which had charged me the day before was, I had then felt, the height of what would be my elephant experience, but now I sit on this tree stump surrounded by six totally wild African elephants! Rumbling of elephants' stomachs and their subtle vocalizations are delightful to ears. Large cow, for some reason, seems to keep other herd members slightly away from me. Lilac-breasted rollers chatter with a series of harsh notes.

3:52 P.M. Feeling more confident, I turn again and for the first time look the big cow directly in the eye. She lifts trunk along my shoulder, resting it there, straight out. Can see prehensile finger at its tip as it searches air for scent, maybe of Bill and Joe, whose presence I can detect in the high grass by glimmer and reflection of telephoto lenses. Sensing that it is time to end encounter, shut mouth and force air up through stomach into nose, trying to imitate the staccato sound Springer describes as the method by which he dispersed animals in similar circumstances. No sooner is sound out of nose than large cow swings around with others behind her, brushing my back as she turns. In moments they disappear into acacia trees where we had first sighted them.

Raise arms in victory sign to Bill and Joe who have gotten to their feet and are starting to run through grass before I can stop them with a shout. Elephants, even though out of sight, are still close—and it is difficult to realize, after my recent experience, that to Bill and Joe they are dangerous animals.

When I reach my friends in the middle of the clearing, no one says anything. We embrace. And then Bill, no longer able to contain himself, shouts, "Fabulous! I can't believe it! No one will! Fabulous!"

"Do you think you got anything?" I ask as we walk through the grass to Elm Tree.

"This time we did," Joe says with a smile.

169

August 16, edge of Nguruman Escarpment

9:00 P.M., camp, edge of Nguruman Escarpment
Dinner over. Dishes done. Sit looking into the fire. Close by hyena whoops. After having called up the elephants today, I have no desire to try conversing with hyena. Darkness and peace have settled on camp. Uncertainty and anxiety, like smoke from the fire, no longer swirl about and cloud our thoughts. Bill and Joe seem refreshed. Who could have blamed them for being discouraged after tramping around Embagai and Olmoti and then discovering that the unicorn of Kilimanjaro was made of snow? And even though we have not yet

seen the real animal, experience with the elephant has convinced them that the seemingly impossible Approach Formula of Rudolf O. Springer is reality.

A lion begins to roar. My companions look up from the fire. We smile at each other. "Tomorrow it's going to be him," says Bill, putting another marshmallow on his stick.

"Or Robert," laughs Joe, then adds, "I'm only kidding."

I think of the lioness kill at Masai Mara. Of the male lion ready to spring, eyes burning, ears flattened, tail whipping the grass. Of the moment of

terror after midnight at Keekorok as the lions lunged, screaming in battle around our tent.

August 17, Monday, 4:30 A.M.
Wake up to lion roaring. The sound seems to be echoing off escarpment, slow paced and dominating the darkness. Seems that only he exists in the world beyond the tent. Think of the lion in Hemingway's story when Macomber's wife asks if the sound is bothering her husband, and he replies, "But I have to kill the thing." Think that I don't have to kill the lion who is ending his call with the typical sigh-wheeze. Think, though I rapidly banish it from mind, that he, however, might kill me.

7:05 A.M. Finish breakfast when Joe says to Bill, "Did you hear the lion last night?"

"Yeah, he was making an awful racket," answers Bill, trying to imitate Hemingway's dialogue.

"Well, I guess we'll have to put a stop to that," says Joe, playing along with game.

"He's a noisy bugger," continues Bill, and then looks over at me. They both start laughing.

"Where did you last hear him? Seriously." I ask.

"That damned roaring's been going on all

night," smiles Bill, again slipping into Hemingway dialogue.

"What are you upset about?" Joe continues, parroting lines from the short story.

"Well, I think it's dreadful," answers Bill.

"Why didn't you waken me," asks Joe. "I would have loved to hear it."

"Robert's got to face the thing," smiles Bill.

"Well, that's what he's here for," answers Joe.

"Yes, but he's nervous." Smiling, Bill looks over at me. "Hearing the thing roar gets on his nerves."

Just then, the lion again starts to call, maybe two miles from camp. The smile leaves my friends' faces. We turn in the direction of the sound.

7:25 A.M. I go to the Land Rover, remove the blue carryon bag, reach into the depths of its contents for the small, cool bottle of Springer's oil formula. Strip down, cold and covered with goose pimples, spread it over the entirety of my body. Then, I carefully reread the copy of the stained and wrinkled pages of the Approach Formula secretly hidden between lining and bottom of the bag.

8:34 A.M., Elm Tree, edge of Nguruman Escarpment

Bill drives slowly across open country, trying to avoid rocks, warthog, and hyena holes, while Joe watches on the left side of Elm Tree, and I on the right. The day is cool and overcast. Yellow fever trees and acacia form complex patterns against the deep purple-blue-gray of the escarpment.

8:45 A.M. Stop Elm Tree and climb onto luggage rack, pan binoculars, scanning slowly in a full circle. No sign of a lion. Now lift binoculars to sky for vulture specks that might indicate a lion kill. Nothing.

12:00 P.M. Sun burns through haze. Most animals, especially predators, are laid up now in bush, or under trees.

3:15 P.M. Lunch late. Doze in Elm Tree parked at edge of plain. Zebra, Thomson's gazelle, and topi.

3:35 P.M. Fly crawling at edge of my mouth—brought awake. Bill and Joe still dozing. Carefully pick up binoculars.

A topi standing on a mound one hundred yards away stamps foreleg nervously and raises head high to stare at a cluster of low acacias. Swing binoculars along acacias. "Lion!" I say softly, and Bill and Joe are awake.

3:45 P.M. Bill eases Elm Tree forward, and we stop seventy yards from the cluster of acacia. Two male lions, four females, and six small cubs form lion pride. Again Karen Blixen's words echo in my ears.

I had seen the royal lion . . . during the midday-siesta, when he reposed contentedly in the midst of his family on the short grass and in the delicate, spring-like shade of the broad Acacia trees of his park of Africa.

Silent, we watch the lions, undoubtedly a pride that has known the reserve life, for they do not seem bothered by Elm Tree or its contents.

3:57 P.M. "What are you waiting for?" asks Bill Wheeler, loading his camera, "go for it."

"Something isn't right," I whisper back to him. "This pride has wandered from one of the reserves." I rack brain for answer to my anxiety. "It's not right. It has to be with completely wild animals. These know Land Rovers and people. I don't feel right about it."

"You're not afraid, are you?" asks Bill.

"Hey, Bill, forget the Hemingway dialogue. This is for real."

"No, seriously," he answers. "I'm not trying to be funny. But one thing is to talk about getting out among them and another thing is doing it."

"I did it with the elephants, didn't I?"

"You did."

"Then trust me. I'm nervous now. I don't feel right about this. Springer said the animals had to be absolutely wild; no zoo animals, or those who had had the slightest contact with white people."

"Robert's right." Joe leans forward from the back seat. "If he doesn't feel right about it, let's look for other lions."

"I suppose so," says Bill. "But that would sure be a beautiful lion to be photographed with."

"Bill," I caution, "remember, even though I've got this oil on my body and formula in my head, we're still in Africa."

5:32 P.M. Sun going down. No further sign of lions. Obviously, pride we encountered has established a territory here and is keeping other lions out. Bill turns Elm Tree around and we start for camp.

10:45 P.M., camp, edge of Nguruman Escarpment

Can't get to sleep. The range of the lion pride we saw today could be very large. Today is August 17; time running short. And a lion encounter must take place before one with unicorns can be attempted. Somewhere, mixed with closer jackal and hyena calls, a lion roars. Hopefully, he is neither part of today's pride nor a reserve animal.

August 18, Tuesday, 6:58 A.M.

Heavy overcast grays the day. Slept fitfully. None of us heard lion all night. Joe and Bill gloomy. Load Elm Tree and decide to drive southwest, toward the Tanzanian border.

10:12 A.M., Elm Tree

Spot large, black-maned lion moving toward herd of zebra. Not a member of yesterday's pride. Makes a handsome picture through Elm Tree's window, gliding through dry grass with dark acacia trees rising up dark behind him, their flat tops silhouetted against fog of escarpment.

10:17 A.M. Excitement fades. Lion looks at the Land Rover as if it were merely another plains animal. Though in a wild area, he also has wandered in from some reserve. Bill and Joe want to photograph him. When zebra catch scent and flee, lion lies down in the grass.

10:45 A.M. Bill and Joe photograph lion. I think—think that perhaps, regardless of Springer's warning, will have to test formula with one of these animals that has wandered out of a reserve. Then it comes on the wind, from out away from the escarpment, to the south, where as far as one can see there is nothing but flat, practically treeless grassland. Black-maned lion lifts his head and answers the distant call of the distant lion. Land in that direction is as flat as men thought earth was before 1492. Where plain curves out of sight, where gray sky meets gray grass, there is something to discover that may revolutionize the study of big cats in the wild.

"Let's go for it," says Bill excitedly, as he puts his camera in case, Elm Tree in gear, and switches on ignition. "Strange that a lion would call at this time of day," he wonders.

11:15 A.M., Elm Tree, plain between Kenya and Tanzania

Worry that we may hit a rock or hole camouflaged by grass. Elm Tree lurches forward across open country, marking trail with twin tracks of bent grass. Slowly, we go on and on, eyes intently searching the sea of ocher-gray.

11:16 A.M. "There they are!" whispers Joe, grabbing my shoulder from the back seat and pointing to the left. Five specks in the grass! With the binoculars, five large lionesses.

"There has to be a male," I say. "There has to be. Bill, stop." Fifty yards from where the lionesses stare at us, there is another shape in the grass. Slowly raises. An immense golden-maned lion!

"Do you see what I see!" Bill Wheeler clears his throat nervously. "I've never seen a lion with a mane that color, and with that much of it."

"Bill," I say, not taking eyes from binoculars. "Drive toward them slowly; we've got to see if they're wild or out of the reserve." Lions are still almost quarter of a mile away.

11:18 A.M. As Elm Tree draws slowly forward, lionesses as well as the lion flatten down into grass, only ears show.

11:21 A.M. Flight distance reached, the lions, one hundred yards away, rise from grass and hurry off, southward, over a low knoll and disappear. I grin at Bill and Joe, who smile back. "Let's plan this now," I say. Bill turns off motor and I climb out of Elm Tree, open the back door, pull out the blue carryon bag, find the bottle of oil, remove my shirt, and pour a small amount of oil into left hand, rub hands together, then work the oil into arm pits, onto face, and in hair. Putting bag back into Land Rover, tell Bill and Joe, "Look, I'm staying here. You circle way around that way." I gesture to the left. "But way around. Give them a mile, then come up behind and slowly herd them this way if you can. But push very slowly, otherwise they'll break off to one side, and if you pressure them too much, this"—I look at the glistening oil traces on my palms—"may not work."

12:17 p.m. Feel like sailor left on deserted island as Elm Tree draws farther and farther away. This will be final test; that is, if my friends are successful in turning back the lions. Feeling of insignificance invades body. Only behind, in the distance, where the escarpment rises, does sky meet anything but flat land. A flock of flamingos passes overhead. Nearby, a lark song is repeated. Where am I? Camargue? Spain? Andalusia? Wyoming? Except that in a short while, hopefully, a pride of African lions will appear and surround me like the big cats in the Los Angeles County Museum surround their waterhole. Here, though, grass is not covered with dust, nor is the background painted, nor will the lions' eyes be made of glass. Bird song comes again, and I squint at the horizon. Should have kept binoculars.

1:07 P.M. Too much time has passed. Elm Tree must be stuck in warthog hole or hung up on a rock, and Land Rover isn't carrying a jack large enough to lift her off or out of either. Maybe they have tried to push the lions too fast. If arrive here at all, perhaps they will be stressed out, aggressive, and unresponsive to formula. Still there is no variation to the horizon. No movement except for grass in the wind.

1:32 P.M. What could have happened? Have to be patient. Far off . . . southeast . . . there is something . . . far in the distance a shape rising out of the grass . . . golden as grass as the sun comes out from behind low clouds and then disappears to again darken landscape . . . movement . . . coming closer . . . no sign of Elm Tree . . . squint and strain eyes even more . . . not playing tricks on me . . . it is coming closer . . . right on course toward me . . . the immense lion of golden mane!

1:41 P.M. Two hundred yards away, lion sees me sitting in grass and stops. There is crosswind. Crouches. I raise up on one knee and voice the first of the three prescribed African lion calls, according to Springer. Lion rises out of grass and in half stalk, half curiosity attitude, slowly approaches. From kneeling position, advancing image seems twice as large as any lion that we have seen from Elm Tree.

Close enough now to see eyes intently concentrating on me. Fifty feet away, still coming slowly. Movement behind him. Far off Elm Tree appears. Lion now twenty feet away. Sun comes out from clouds to back-light mane. Never seen lion with such a magnificent mane. Here, perhaps, in such open country, it receives little pulling and tear loss from thornbushes. Can see his pupils. Give second of Springer's vocalizations, lips back, pulling tightly around face. Lion stops five feet away. Heart pounds. Mind pounds with Karen Blixen's words.

In their build, carriage and movements, lions possess a greatness, a majesty, which positively instills terror in the human being and makes one feel later that everything else is so trivial—thousands of generations of unrestricted supreme authority, and one is oneself set back 6,000 generations—suddenly comes to feel the mighty power of nature, when one looks it right in the eyes. —Karen Blixen

Feel he could flee as easily as attack. Can hear sniffing in as he absorbs my odor.

1:44 P.M. Lion takes a step forward. Then another, and another, now two feet away. Keeping mouth shut, I give third low vocalization. Lion's face is now an inch from my own, so near I cannot see sky. Feel his breath on my chest. So close, eyes can't focus on him.

Now when he turns head sharply to look over shoulder at Elm Tree, fifty yards away, mane hair touches and tickles my nose. Bite lip to keep from sneezing. Lion backs off, then slowly walks around me. Behind now. Carefully peer around to see him sniffing tire tracks that led me to him and left me at this spot. Glances over shoulder at Elm Tree, but takes no further notice of me. Turns around twice in tight circles to the left before laying down. I sit down in dry grass.

2:00 P.M. Bill has patiently driven to within fifty yards when lion looks toward Elm Tree. Growls. Slowly, I raise hand to indicate that Land Rover should stop.

2:25 P.M. Have spent almost an hour with lion, which rests with head on paws. Now and then rubs side of his face and ear against the ground and growls, but not aggressively. Could there be an imbedded foxtail in ear that now, having festered and healed, causes him to scratch it? Has looked at Elm Tree repeatedly, but at me only twice, and then seemingly with an air of disdain.

2:42 P.M. Lion suddenly raises his head and stares over right shoulder. Issues low growl. Cautiously turn to left until five lionesses, grouped closely together, heads held high with curiosity, can be seen watching us, but do not approach.

3:00 P.M. Sun again breaks from clouds. Some pride members are sitting up, unwilling to approach, seemingly waiting for lion to join them. Lion stands, stretches, and circles around me. Try to watch him out of the corner of my eye.

No animal, however fast, has greater speed than a charging lion over a distance of a few yards. It is speed faster than thought—faster always than escape.—Beryl Markham

Slowly raise the camera and take one photograph of the lionesses. Lion snarls at sound of motor drive. Cautiously lower camera. Will leave picture-taking to Bill's and Joe's lenses, which extend from both sides of Elm Tree.

3:05 P.M. Lion does a turn around me, testing wind, which is now blowing northeast, toward the distant escarpment. Then settles back into grass. I raise up on one knee and he pays no more attention to me than if I were a stump or rock. Now start to relax. Place right hand chest high, close against body, and prudently wave to Bill and Joe, whose cameras still flash reflections from Elm Tree's windows. Breeze vibrates grass that months before had been cut short, first by zebra and wildebeest, and then gazelle during the migration that has now reached Oloololo Escarpment and is returning in this direction to the Serengeti. Lion's mane also ruffled by the slight wind. I lay back into the stiff, dry grass and stare up at gray cloud passing overhead. Now and then the sun breaks through the overcast to warm my face.

3:15 P.M. Sit up. Lion has not moved. Looking slowly around, see that the lionesses have changed position, gone eastward toward a stand of yellow grass, and face a herd of zebra a quarter of a mile away. Carefully, fan out and begin the hunt.

Zebra barks. Golden mane of lion sweeps up from the grass as he fixes on zebra herd. Between it and us, the lionesses can barely be seen in dry grass. Several of pride now and then look back toward us.

Not taking eyes from them, lion gets to his feet and stretches, at the same time yawning to show a broken canine tooth. Looks at me, licks his lips, then casually starts to circle out to the right. His concentration, as he passes, produces electricity between us. Right now, if just a single wish were mine, how I would join him instead of being a human sitting here, dressed in a silly suit, with a cold piece of metal in my hands.

4:03 P.M. Lion now far off, having circled wide around the zebra, not invading their flight distance.

Hear Elm Tree's motor come to life.

4:10 P.M. Land Rover stops beside me. Bill and Joe disembark, smiling. "Praise Rudolf Q. Springer," says Bill joyfully, "and forgive me for ever doubting him."

"It's 'O' not 'Q' Springer. Were you able to get anything?" I ask Joe, knowing that Bill, who insists on using 64 ASA film with large lenses on this dark day and a slow shutter speed, will have nothing but blurred images.

"I got everything you could wish for," grins Joe. "And I shot with my camera and with your other one just in case one has a malfunction.

"It's beyond belief!" exclaims Bill, his face beaming with amazement. "It's totally beyond belief!"

"They're hunting," I point to the zebra, then climb onto Elm Tree's roof with the binoculars. Even from roof of the Land Rover, the lionesses are practically undetectable, flattened and pressed to become one with grass. Male is now on far side of the zebra, who watch as he slowly walks toward them.

Zebra stallion in front of herd, facing lion, while mares and a young colt line up behind him, assuming characteristic equine alert position. As lion strides nearer, stallion barks sharply. This seems to cause lion to increase gait. Zebra stallion whirls, as does herd, turning toward us and the flattened forms in the dry grass. Panicked zebra gallop frantically. In an instant, lionesses leaping up and dashing into them. Movement everywhere. Can't concentrate on any one figure. Can the lionesses? Then zebra are running off—herd intact—as the lion pride gaze after them. A failed hunt.

Male approaches one of the females. They rub heads, bodies.

"Are you going to try to interact with the whole pride?" asks Bill.

Pull at my khakis. Body oil and sweat cause cloth to stick uncomfortably to me. "I doubt if they'll all come to me. Why don't you go back for the tent. We can camp here with them tonight. As soon as I see you on the horizon, I'll try and call them up. I'd rather you be here with the Land Rover. If they all crowd around me and one gets aggressive, you can drive them off. If we don't get any pictures today, if it doesn't work, at least we can be here with them early in the morning and try for it then. But that's all. We have to start for Entaskera by noon. Tomorrow's the nineteenth of August. Only a week left to find and study unicorns. . ."

4:30 P.M. Land Rover has disappeared and lions are bedded down in grass. Overhead a trio of Egyptian vultures, white under the canopy of gray.

5:15 P.M. Light beginning to go. One lioness stands, stretches, then another. This is the same

kind of synchronized resting-waking group behavior that I have observed with horses in Camargue.

5:19 P.M. Head high, one of the lionesses begins walking away, toward escarpment. Other members of the pride follow, including golden-maned male. No sight or sound of Elm Tree. Soon pride will be too distant to attempt to call them up. And what guarantee is there that we will find them in the morning? However, the thought of being surrounded—literally face to face—by six completely wild, adult lions, without Bill and Joe nearby in the Land Rover, makes me anxious.

5:22 P.M. Put hands to mouth and voice first of Springer's lion-approach vocalizations. Lead lioness stops and looks back over shoulder. Golden-maned male immediately turns and starts in my direction. Pride follows.

august 18, edge of Nguruman Escarpment

5:25 P.M. Pride of six lions now fifty feet away, advancing faster now. Give second vocalization.

5:26 P.M. Surrounded by pride. Lions behind, in front, and on either side of me. Male stands two feet away, looking toward escarpment. Suddenly feel hot breath on back of head. Then cold nose of lioness touches my neck. Male turns in my direction and snarls. Lioness behind me growls, then can hear her pads pressing the grass as she backs off.

5:40 P.M. Pride has settled into grass around me. All intently stare toward escarpment. Darkness coming fast. Where are Bill and Joe? Now too late for photography. Each second is taken observing. Too much to watch with so many animals at such close range. Do not feel as confident as earlier alone with male. Quiet, except for the wind and the "pleet, pleet, pleet, pleet" whistle of a Harlequin quail.

6:15 P.M. Lions have risen in direction of escarpment. Faces tense and heads become immobile. It is now difficult to see their forms in the falling darkness or the lines on the pages of this notebook. Two jackal appear fifty yards to right. Toward escarpment a hyena whoops.

6:28 P.M. Lions appear restless. Suddenly, all are moving around me, some so close that their tails swish against my head, back, and shoulders. Where are Bill and Joe?

6:32 P.M. Sound of Elm Tree? Cup my hands to ears and look in same direction that the pride is now facing. Yes, it is the Land Rover. Pinpoints of headlights in distance.

6:41 P.M. Lions scatter as Land Rover draws closer. All have disappeared into darkness except the male, who stands at my shoulder until Elm Tree is fifty feet away, then he turns to vanish after the pride.

"I thought we'd never find you," says Joe, climbing out of Elm Tree.

"I thought you'd never come," I answer. "You missed some great shots. The entire pride was here."

"We saw their eyes!" exclaims Bill. "They were right around you and didn't do anything?"

"Just as Springer describes it. Just as though I hadn't been here," I answer. "Except for a lioness who had her nose on my neck until the male growled at her."

"We got lost," says Bill, as he walks to the back of Elm Tree, opens the door, and pulls out tent. "As soon as the sun started to drop, we kept losing the tire tracks in the grass to lead us back here."

"We thought we'd never find you," says Joe. "And even with Springer's formula, I was worried."

As we stumble about, setting up the tent in the darkness, I tell my friends of experience with pride.

10:50 P.M. Feels good to be under the blankets on my mattress. "I can hardly wait until tomorrow," yawns Joe. "To photograph you in the center of the pride."

"We've got to get up early," says Bill, who despises early rising.

Somewhere nearby, jackals howl to remind me of coyotes in California, and far, far off toward the escarpment, a lion starts to roar. Sleep comes easy.

August 19, Wednesday, 11:30 A.M., plain, Kenya–Tanzania

Lions have vanished as if from face of the earth. Have spent all morning searching in every direction. No sight of them since last night when the pride sat around me and Elm Tree arrived to send them scampering into the blackness. No sound from them since last night, just before I went to sleep. Bill and Joe terribly disappointed, as am I. Tell them that we are fortunate to have obtained the material now stored in film cartridges, notebooks, and memories. One hundred years have passed since Springer's expedition, and since anyone has enjoyed, and lived through, such experience.

12:57 P.M. Return to tent and pack up camp. As Bill pulls Elm Tree forward, Joe and I notice a large spot of oil on grass. Throughout trip have had to continually pump oil into Elm Tree's gearbox. At Amboseli defective seal was repaired, and again at Keekerok, but still the oil leaks. Now Bill crawls under the Land Rover while Joe prepares pump. Bill curses mechanics who have worked on gearbox in Zaire, Uganda, Tanzania, and Kenya.

Leave camp to look for and press wildflowers.

1:45 P.M. Secretary bird runs and then low glides alongside Elm Tree as we bounce toward escarpment, which is still miles away. Joe and I sit on Elm Tree's luggage rack. Sun that has broken through the clouds warms our necks while the breeze plays over faces. Joe and I look at one another and smile. Words unnecessary.

2:10 P.M. Still there is no sign of lions. Now and then, I drop my boot down over windscreen, signaling Bill to stop. Then he joins us on the luggage rack while we scan grass for lions and sky for vultures that might indicate if and where they are laying up on a kill.

3:25 P.M., edge of Nguruman Escarpment

Reach edge of escarpment and find road that will lead us back up into the mountains to Entaskera.

4:20 P.M., Nguruman Forest

Earth on road reddens to deep red-orange. Walls of green forest tower up on either side.

5:30 P.M. Arrive at point in road where Masai gave us directions on Thursday, August 13. Seems that two years have passed since then.

5:34 P.M. Road forks with left split returning to twist and wind down out of Loita Hills to the main highway to Narok and on to Nairobi. Right fork, smaller road with grass growing in center, to Entaskera.

5:40 P.M. Drop down into arroyo. Three Masai boys herding cattle block the road. Colors of orange-red road now cast in pink from going sun. Cattle also rose-colored. Boys wear bright red tunics. "Jambo," we shout to them.

Boys raise hands to wave, and in soft bird sounds, sing, "Jambo!" back. This is Africa, but colors are Gauguin's.

6:10 P.M. Pass manyatta on right. See movement in twilight. Masai dancing. Red-and-yellow-striped blanket wrapped around him, a handsome man of middle age approaches car. "Jambo," he says, then, in English, "Welcome, my name is Daniel. Do you wish to see the dancing?"

Joe and Bill conceal small tape recorders in their pockets; we tuck cameras away under our arms, lock Elm Tree's doors, and in fading light walk to the manyatta. Several teenage boys continue dancing, leaping, springing, pronking straight up like impala, shoulders, neck, and heads arching back when they reach the end of their soar, returning to earth with a slap of their feet.

Daniel tells us in a voice as soft as wild honey that the celebration is in honor of one of the morani who is becoming an elder. He asks if we wish to photograph. When we say yes, he leads us to the doorway of chief's hut, which is typically dome shaped and plastered with cow dung. Daniel enters. Wait and in seconds he is back, beckoning us to enter. Inside of the hut in complete darkness except for flicker of fire. There are no windows, and a wall that runs along the doorway shuts out light from single entrance. Chief sits across the room. In front of him the most lovely of Masai girls sterilizes a milk gourd by placing hot coals into it to kill bacteria produced by milk.

We greet the chief and the man who sits beside him, smile, and shake hands. There is only the odor of acrid smoke, the same that years before in Spain I became accustomed to while living with a gypsy family. Price of taking photographs, even in this primitive off-the-track village, is 200 shillings. Bill pays and then attempts to photograph girl and fire. The flames flash glow on the faces, wrinkled and wise, of the old men. From the moment we

entered the manyatta, with singing and dancing, the courtyards of women, children, and cattle, we are living a scene from *King Solomon's Mines* or *Mogambo*, except instead of Stewart Granger or Clark Gable, this is our movie.

Finally, Joe and I, with Daniel, leave the hut.

6:40 P.M. Singing and chanting in ears, splendid figures of morani springing into the air, can't determine if I am in Africa—or in heaven.

7:20 P.M. Daniel's manyatta

As we leave the manyatta and dancing, chief tells us we will always be welcome here. He has the gentle, wise expression of a good man. Daniel says that he can take us into Forest of the Lost Children, to the hot springs and falls. But tell him we must first find Rafael, who had been recommended by Ben Kipeno at the Oloololo Escarpment, and by Simon Makallah. As Daniel climbs into Elm Tree only then do I realize that he has the same name as my faithful Daniel who probably now sits in the evening at Cañada Grande, worrying that I will never return to Spain from Africa.

7:25 P.M., near Entaskera

Turn right off main road and one hundred yards farther come to another manyatta. Daniel approaches first boma and asks for Rafael. Cattle, goats, and sheep, with their bells, sound in the twilight as Daniel leads us to far boma. Woman is pulling stick and thorn branches into place to block corral entrance. We climb over a fence. Daniel motions for us to wait, respectfully clears throat, and enters hut. Hear muffled voices. Daniel returns and says that Rafael has asked us inside. Start to enter, but so dark that Bill suggests we request Rafael to come outside, so that we can see more clearly the face of the man we have come to meet.

Shortly, Rafael appears. Taller than any of us. Gold-rimmed eyeglasses give him air and appearance of a black Harvard professor. After shaking hands in greeting, he says, "You will have to excuse me. We have been drinking, as you must note." He laughs. "It would be more desirable if we talk in the morning."

As Daniel directs us to his own boma, reflect on Rafael, once a sergeant major in Kenya's army, now living in a cow dung hut in Entaskera. Daniel invites us to spend night inside his home. We thank him but pitch tent in the darkness fifty yards away. Later he brings us wood and an immense log; says to care for the fire through the night for there are many leopard and buffalo in forest. Once tent is up and we are heating two cans of chili beans, ocher-colored dog creeps up and lies close to the fire. I think of Kizzy waiting for me at Cañada Grande.

9:39 P.M., Daniel's manyatta

Rain patters tent. Feel safe inside. Occasional sheep or cattle bell can be heard from the manyatta. In the morning we will meet with Rafael and Daniel to plan foot safari. So far have said nothing to either of them of Nentikobe—the unicorn.

August 20, Thursday, 2:05 A.M., Daniel's manyatta

Awaken repeatedly. Unlike the plain below, here there are few night sounds. Feeling of serenity. Only a hyena whoops in the far distance. Rain has stopped.

3:24 A.M. Start, wide-eyed awake, from dream of Masai boys in red tunics with herd of unicorns. Of Masai girl, Daniel's sister, decorated with flowers instead of beads, sitting on rocks near a stream from which drinks a black unicorn . . . Drift back to sleep.

6:00 A.M. Wake to rain drops pelting tent. Expect sounds of cattle or human voices from the boma, but outside are only the voices of awakening birds. Fear the rain, but reason tells me it will stop with rising sun.

6:45 A.M. Joe is awake. Says he can hardly wait to get out of tent. Bill, in the dim light, face so pale, his hands crossed over chest, appears like a corpse laid out for a wake.

7:00 A.M. Bill awakens with a low growl and unzips tent. Gray outside. At sound of crying baby, think of the Forest of the Lost Children. Joe and I dress. Suddenly, rain starts falling. Back inside the tent to write. Can barely stand waiting. Anxious to have planning over and see the Elm Tree disappearing behind as Masai, with their loads, plunge into the forest toward the falls, leaving manyatta behind. A pair of tropical bulbuls choruses. One utters three rapid, clear bell-like whistles and is answered with a croaking "kwee." Combined, they sound like a squeaky pump.

8:15 A.M. Gas stove breaks as we prepare breakfast. Daniel arrives. Says he is going off to find Rafael.

9:36 A.M. During past few days we have continually discussed trying to convince Masai to use their handsome donkeys as pack animals for safari. Donkeys, with black leg, dorsal stripes, and soft gray-mauve coats, remind me of the more delicate Somali wild ass. Rafael arrives with Daniel. "As I told you last night," he says. "And you must excuse me for not attending to you then. Daniel is a fine man, and he can take you to the falls, and then down the escarpment to Lake Natron if you have time to go there. You should need five or six men?"

"Couldn't we take donkeys to carry some of the gear?" questions Bill.

"Impossible," laughs Rafael, who today makes an even more charming impression than last evening. "They are not trained to wear a bridle. Here we put loads on their backs, but we herd them. They are not accustomed to the deep forest. The first time they heard a buffalo, or an elephant, they would run away with all of your supplies. That is impossible."

Now I feel is right time. Look directly into Rafael's kind eyes and ask, "Do you know the Nentikobe?"

Rafael again bursts into laughter. "First you want to take donkeys into the forest, and now you want to know about the Nentikobe, something that does not exist. Who told you about that animal?"

"Many people," I reply. "What do you know about it?"

"Some say it is made of metal. Very shiny and very hard. It is a legend used to keep children from wandering into the forest. So you are looking for the Nentikobe."

I glance at Daniel, who smiles nervously, then casts his eyes toward the ground. A hill babbler whistles its clear, two-note call.

"You will need one man to stay here and watch your Land Rover," says Rafael, obviously not wanting to continue the conversation about unicorns. "You will need Daniel and four porters to carry your things. You will have to buy supplies. You will need a goat for these men to eat, and you will buy another along the way. Daniel can take charge of these things today, and you should be ready to leave in the morning." He raises his walking stick and smiles. "So you are looking for the Nentikobe. I have never met a white man who knew about this. That shows even the deepest secrets and legends of the forest have found their way to the world beyond there." He swings his stick in the direction above the treetops. "Well, where you are going is a very beautiful place. Daniel is a trustworthy man, and he will take you there."

With Rafael and Daniel, Bill negotiates wages for the porters for first five days, which will be increased for any time beyond that. I suggest that instead of four porters and Daniel, that we take an extra man. Remind Bill and Joe that on their foot safaris to Tanzania, they often had to carry heavy loads that took away enjoyment, time, and energy for field observation.

10:05 A.M. Rafael is gone, and Bill and Daniel are reviewing list of supplies that will be needed for a seven-day safari, which will take us to the falls, down the escarpment to Lake Natron, and as close as we can walk to Ol Doinyo Lengai before having to turn back. When the list and initial arrangements have been completed, I call Daniel aside. There is mystery in Daniel Ole Mengoru's dark Masai eyes, flashing and dimming like zebra in the night. Of one thing only I am certain—he has seen the Nentikobe—the unicorn.

"Daniel," I begin, "it is important that you tell me the truth. Have you seen the Nentikobe? I know you have, I was sure you had when Rafael laughed and you looked down at the ground."

"You heard what Rafael said," Daniel answers in his soft voice. "It is a legend that is used to keep children out of the forest. You know in Africa there are many legends."

"Please, Daniel, I know you are a good man, and a good man would try to protect the Nentikobe. I know you have seen it, I can tell from your eyes," I plead. "Please tell me, it is very important. It is my reason for coming here."

"If people thought it existed they would come here to try and capture it," he answers. "Poachers would come, like they come for the ivory, and try to kill it. But how can they, if it is only a legend?"

"Come with me." I motion to him, and he followed to the edge of the clearing to the wall of jungle, a hundred yards away from Elm Tree and the boma. Then as he stares in puzzlement, I put hands to mouth, cupping out palms and softly voice the first of Springer's sounds for calling up a stag unicorn.

"Then you know," says Daniel, a smile sparkles from his teeth and dark eyes. "But why do you want to see them, it will only bring other people here? Bad people. Some good, perhaps, but some bad."

Place my hand on the red-and-yellow-striped blanket slung over his shoulder. "Daniel, there will always be good people, as well as bad people. If more good people are aware of how beautiful Nentikobe is, and how rare he is, something may be done to help save him. Maybe they can stop the forests from being cleared where he lives and help stop the poachers from coming here, even though Nentikobe, as you know, has magical ways and can escape most bad men. But before we can get close to him, you will first have to wash this in the hot spring near the tree of the Laibons, and then in the water of the falls." I take hold of his spear.

"So you know about all of these things. But how does a white man know these things? My people say there was only one. The man with hair of fire, but that was before my father's time, and before his father's time, and before that."

"The man with hair like fire," I say aloud. What had Springer's great-great-niece written: screwball red-haired uncle. And so . . . this was the final proof. So Rudolf O. Springer had been at this very manyatta. "What do you know of that man with hair the color of fire?" I ask Daniel.

"Nothing more than that," answers Daniel. "That he was a friend of the Nentikobe's. That he lived with our people. He was a friend of our people. He did not come here to shoot the animals like all the rest. He came just to look at them, and to live with them. He must have been like a white Laibon, if there is such a thing."

"When did you last see the Nentikobe? Please, Daniel, it is important, we have very little time."

Daniel gazes into my eyes. "You are a good man, Robert. Yes, it is in your eyes. The Nentikobe, if you mean it no harm, you may see it almost when you wish. But what of your friends?"

"They mean it no harm. And what of the Masai who are going with us?" I question.

"First, it is better that you say nothing of this to them. Some are very superstitious and would not accompany us if they knew why you are here. Others are good men, but there are temptations if they see and know how to find the Nentikobe. It is better to keep them with no temptations. If James, who is my brother, comes with us, you trust him. David, my nephew may also be trusted. But to the others . . ." he puts his finger to his lips. "You say nothing. Besides," his face breaks into a handsome smile, "besides, they do not speak English, the others, that is, so you could not talk to them anyway. But do not mention the name of that animal unless we are alone. Now I must start to try and find these men for the safari, and try to buy the maize and rice and the other things we will need. Seven days is not a short time."

Not simply wanting to sit around the manyatta all day, I ask Daniel, "I suppose there is no chance that we could try and look for Nentikobe today, close to here, while you make those arrangements for the safari?"

Daniel stops and jabs the handle point of his spear into the ground. "That is possible, but it will have to be from a distance, from your car, with those." He points to the binoculars around my neck. "You must do exactly as I say, for James and David are coming with me and cannot accompany you. I will make you a map and you go there. You wait." He points to his watch. "You go there and you sit very quietly on the top of your car, and at four o'clock in the afternoon, maybe a little later, but very little, the Nentikobe will appear. He does so every day if there is no danger. But you must not make that sound to try and bring him to you, and you must not try and walk closer to him. You stay in your car, and you will see him. Do you have pen and paper?"

I give Daniel my notebook and ballpoint.

"You take this road," he speaks as he draws on the paper. "This is the road on which you came here from Masai Mara. You follow this until another one smaller takes this direction, that is only fifteen minutes from here in your car. That is to the right. You follow that road for not a long distance and the dirt of the road will be very red. Then there will be a mountain on one side of the road and a mountain on the other side. The mountain on the left side of that road will be very red. But very red. Then you come to the trees. They are very big yellow fever trees on the left side of the road you are traveling upon. You stop at these trees. There are also these orange flowers. Tall ones. Yes, you should be at the tree at, let us say, two o'clock. And you wait, very quietly. Like you were waiting for a lion or an elephant. You must tell your friends to be very quiet. And I would suggest that only one of you wait on the top of your car. And you will see, at the time he will appear on the side of the red mountain. You will see him through the trees. Nentikobe will appear. And if

you are very still, he will do his dance. This you will see for sure. But when you return to this place," he pushes the end of the spear deeper into the ground, "you must not speak of this to any person. If you do, we will have a very difficult time finding men to carry our things for the safari."

Reaching Elm Tree, Bill gives Daniel money for the supplies and porters. For seven days Daniel will receive one thousand shillings, each of the five porters, seven hundred shillings, two hundred shillings for the goat, and five hundred shillings for supplies.

2:20 P.M. As try to sleep siesta, Masai Mara migration stampedes my mind. Tens of thousands of hoofed, horned animals, but no trace of the Nentikobe. Could the tree where man was born be the one beneath which the last *Unicornuus africanus* died?

Lion Tail

3:45 P.M., Elm Tree, Loita Hills

Daniel's directions perfect. Fork in the road. The earth becoming very deep red. Orange, lion tail flowers. And the stand of yellow fever trees on the left. The steep red layers of deep red rocky mountainside to the left seen through the branches of fever trees. Pair of slate-colored bulbuls duet, one uttering four bell-like notes, followed immediately by the second bird giving a double croak. Suddenly, one of the bulbuls calls, "krrrr" in alarm.

3:52 P.M. Joe is fifty yards down the road photographing a turaco. Bill sits in Land Rover. I stand on luggage rack, waiting. Look at watch. Almost four o'clock. Joe should be inside with Bill. Start to turn to call him when . . . it appears. Nentikobe! Oh, Daniel was right.

The unicorn runs along ledge of deep red rock. Whistle softly through teeth, Joe looks up and I motion for him to drop down in grass at roadside, then softly say, "Bill, it's here."

"Where?" he whispers back.

"Stay still," I say and watch through binoculars. First African unicorn! One of the most magnificent stag unicorns have seen anywhere! Dark eyes indicate that it is a young animal. Continues running along ledge, parallel to Elm Tree. Slowly pick up camera with 500-millimeter lens. Side of mountain is very dark. Hopefully, with 400 ASA film and white unicorn, will be enough light.

Stag stops directly opposite Land Rover. Stares at me for an instant. Begins display. *Cymothoe* butterfly flashes red, out of focus in binoculars. In years of concentrated unicorn observation never have I seen an animal so caught up in ritual, nor so exaggerated and dramatic in executing it. Could it be that *Unicornuus africanus* is so different from other races? Rears. Lunges. Tosses head and mane. Rolls eyes. And all in relatively small area. The only sounds now are a pair of Hadada ibis calling back and forth, from one side of the road to the other, and the sharp smacking of stag's hooves against red rock.

"I can't see anything," whispers Bill. "I'm too low. What's going on?"

Slowly setting down the camera, I again pick up binoculars and inch my way upward to a standing position. Unicorn seems totally unaffected by our presence. In fact, that is not true,—he seems to be displaying directly toward us. Never have seen any animals so dramatically animated in ritual.

Hearing the door of Elm Tree creak open, I look down to see Bill blinking up at me. "Is it out there? Robert, I can't see anything."

"Don't move," I whisper down to him.

"That's not fair," he whispers back, now louder.

"Remember what happened at the wildebeest crossing?" I answer. "Remember what happened

when Joe and I wanted to get closer, and you refused to move. Now's the time to stay still. Stay still!"

Unicorn is ending display. Rears slightly, then does half turn, dashes along ledge of red rock, and leaps down to streambed to disappear into vegetation.

Let binoculars lay against chest and wave for Joe to return to the Land Rover. "All I could see was some flashes of white through the brush. What did it look like?" complains Bill.

"Like a unicorn," I smile down at him. "Sorry to have told you to stay still like that, but your movement might have caused him to flee sooner. Don't worry, you'll see one."

"Boy, that was great!" exclaims Joe as he reaches Elm Tree. "That was really great!"

"Did you see it? You couldn't see it from there," says Bill.

"I could see it from between the trees. There was a clearing in the brush," replies Joe. "I saw it, and if I don't see another thing the rest of this trip, that's enough for me. Wow!"

6:15 P.M., Daniel's manyatta

As twilight falls at Daniel's manyatta, I feel transformed, standing among his family. Feel as if had 10,000 milligrams of niacin inside me, though instead of the flush, I experience a glow that persists, within my being and without. Anxiousness is gone, feel removed and distant, and at the same time very much in touch with all I see, breathe, and hear. What is the reason for this high? Certainly not the brew that the Masai have made of mysterious roots and herbs from deep forest. Or is spectacular display of unicorn, and proof of its existence here, cause for this rare state? I think not. I think the glow is simply and merely Africa, fitting this piece of myself into that one empty space in the puzzle of my existence.

9:25 P.M. Daniel brings more wood for fire. Bill and Joe are happy. One need not listen to their words, but only to look into their eyes to see it. Foot safaris into Olmoti and Embagai were in part grueling tests of endurance in which my friends carried sixty-pound packs, often on hands and knees, through buffalo trails and up the steep crater sides. Forced marches when fatigue and hurry interfered with taking time out to study the creatures and the land. Tomorrow they will be able not only to touch Africa, but to take time to see,

hear, and smell her. This is not to deny that today's sighting of the unicorn does not have something to do with the aura that one can also sense
around them.

10:15 P.M. Drifting off in sleep when it comes.
Haunting and wonderful and far away. Like cat
meow and raven call combined. The voice of the
Hadada ibis. Far overhead. Then going away.
Away. Away . . .

August, 21, Friday, 11:42 A.M., Daniel's manyatta
Here I sit next to the eight duffel bags that contain our provisions. Supposed to have started into
forest at daybreak, but two of the Masai contracted
as porters by Daniel yesterday have not arrived.
Bill, Joe, and Daniel have driven off to find them or
to hire others. Delay is disappointing, but after
having lived in Spain for almost thirty years, it's
not surprising that here things also have a way of
going wrong at the last minute.

Sit on a blue tarp, lean against duffel bags. Behind me stand several morani, their hair colored
red and painted leg decorations remain from the
ceremony of two days ago. They stand cross-
legged, with water gourds wedged between their
inner thighs, spears stuck in ground. They chew
something like tobacco, now and then spit. Another boy arrives. Politely they shake hands. For
the first time flies are annoying.

12:03 P.M. Civilization seems far away, so far
beyond the green hills. Does it really exist? Was it
a dream? Is this paradise the only reality I have
ever known? The sharp smell of the campfire and
of the Masai, their soft voices, the continual sound
of the spear ends stabbed into the ground. The
cuckoo and bulbul birds calling nearby. Morani
standing, gazing off toward the green hill. The
rounded shapes of the huts against the sky. The
porters sitting or squatting, waiting for the safari to
move. The white man in old khaki Spanish army
uniform, leaning against the duffel bags waiting for
the safari to begin. The screeching of turacos. The
piping of the doves. The pump song of tropical
bulbuls.

12:15 P.M. Ears plead for the sound of Elm Tree.
Anxiousness to get going is overpowering. Child,
wrapped in a blue cloth, runs down the hill, crying. Rain begins to fall lightly. A tall, slim old man
walks toward the fire. His right ear hole is
stretched by a Vaseline bottle. Boys approach him
and respectfully shake hands. I can only smile.
One of the boys throws short stick through the air,
whirring at an imaginary target. Now there is the
sound of a motor. Elm Tree. The waiting is over.

1:20 P.M. Help porters hoist the backpacks onto
their shoulders."You're going to enjoy this a little
more," I say to Bill and Joe. They now are carrying
only their cameras, and smile, recalling the agoniz-
ing heavy packs carried at Olmoti and Embagai. I
then look over at Daniel. "Let's go, Daniel, but tell
the men to stay together and that we aren't going
too fast." Daniel speaks to the porters in Masai,
and the safari begins.

1:51 P.M., *Loita Hills*

Reach top of first hill and look back at manyatta. Oval domes of houses appear no larger than halved thrush eggs.

2:11 P.M. Meet Masai boy carrying leg of roast beef. Stop, and porters take meat and cut from it. Sit around and eat. Everyone tired. No sound but the chomping of jaws.

3:20 P.M., approaching Forest of Lost Children.

Cross grassy, open areas, and then are absorbed into the darkness of primordial forest. Smells of damp vegetation and fragrance of flowers. Scents change with whims of breeze.

An African Native Forest is a mysterious region. You ride into the depths of an old tapestry, in places faded and in others darkened with age, but marvellously rich in green shades. You cannot see the sky at all in there, but the sunlight plays in many strange ways, falling through the foliage. The grey fungus, like long drooping beards, on the trees, and the creepers hanging down everywhere, give a secretive, recondite air to the Native Forest. . . .

The air in the forest was cool like water, and filled with the scent of plants, and in the beginning of the long rains when the creepers flowered, you rode through sphere after sphere of fragrance.
—Karen Blixen

3:45 P.M. Forest opens. Proceed along grassy corridor. Climb hill and stop. Spears plunge into ground, packs drop off, and we drop into tall grass.

Daniel points out Colobus monkey, a speck of black and white in the top of green forest.

3:55 P.M. Clearing ends. Back into trees. Follow animal trail. Vegetation so thick in some places that we must bend over to pass through dark tunnels cut in the forest by buffalo. Obvious if buffalo encountered here, could be no escape. Buffalo signs everywhere. Even in open areas it is impossible to ignore the danger. Rely only on Daniel and porters' keen sense to protect us. Remember Bror Blixen's words:

On one side of us the plain lay empty, on the other was wood. We were walking along the trees, a short bellow, and the buffalo was right on us. No one who has not had a similar experience can imagine with what extraordinary swiftness the attack is made.

4:03 P.M. Walking grassy corridor. Smell of smoke comes and goes. Manyatta, where men will buy goat, must be nearby. Start to round a finger of forest when porters suddenly throw off packs. Spears ready and sparkling in hazy sun. Before us, seventy yards away, at edge of forest, stands massive Cape buffalo. Head high, nose up, whites of eyes showing, horns curving out against green of forest. Holds his ground. Bigger than any we have seen in the parks, or is it because now we are looking at him on his level and not from Elm Tree? One of Masai whirls karry-knocker (small stick) at buffalo, which charges off to side, then whirls, snorts, and again faces us. Adrenaline cascading.

Two more sticks are thrown. Buffalo turns and crashes into forest. Masai, spears cocked back, advance slowly toward edge of forest. Hear buffalo moving behind wall of green. Look around for a tree, a bush, anything behind which I can hide or into which I can climb. Remember Peter Matthiessen commenting that at time of a buffalo attack, the trees that one rushes toward are either too small to be climbed or if they are large enough, branches are too high to be reached.

4:05 P.M. The Masai have lowered spears, and we help load packs onto their backs. Leave the open area, and again enter dense forest, and duck into a buffalo tunnel. A trace of gray smoke snakes across the red earth of the trail. Manyatta is very near.

4:45 P.M. Stop a few hundred yards from manyatta while Bill and Daniel go ahead to buy goat. Joe and I sit on rocks with porters. Two Hadada ibis, crying, glide overhead toward marsh and forest that lie beyond manyatta.

5:15 P.M. Bill returns and we start into swamp. Grass and reeds higher than our heads. Masai shout and clap hands to hopefully frighten buffalo. Reeds become higher and thicker. Frightened. Here no escape.

5:25 P.M. Tall reeds end in bog. Stretch of black, stagnant water, fifty feet across, lies ahead. No way around it, Daniel says. Must wade through. Promised myself would not take foolish chances on this trip. Everyone has warned, "Keep out of still water. Whatever you do, don't go into still water. Bilharziasis." Tired. Campsite supposedly only quarter mile away. Masai porters now crossing water, which swirls up black around knees.

Look over Bill and Joe taking off shoes and socks. "We shouldn't do this," I say, as they remove their trousers. "It's crazy."

"If you're going to get to the falls," says Bill as he starts to wade into the bog, pants held high in one hand while he attempts to keep balance with the other, "there is no other choice."

"But everyone says it's crazy," I answer. "Daniel, isn't there another way around?"

"This is the narrowest place to cross," he replies.

What to do? Call one of the Masai and give him a hundred shillings to carry me across? Bilharziasis gets to the brain and kidneys. Everyone knows it is one of the most terrible of tropical diseases.

Others nearing far side of the bog as I slip off boots, socks, and trousers and step into the sucking black muck. *Hopefully, Springer's oil*, I think, *also works against the* Bilharziasis cercaria.

8:35 P.M., camp, edge of the Forest of the Lost Children

Beyond marsh there is a hill from which an immense tree rises. Signs of many campfires under tree, around which has been constructed a barrier of thorn branches. Below tree stretches a meadow of tall grass bordered by forest. In middle of clearing is another immense tree, similar to the one where Daniel and the porters are now making their camp. Pitch tent fifty yards down from them at the edge of meadow. Sixty yards to our left, Daniel shows me the hot spring described by Springer and in which Masai spears must be washed before we set out for falls in the morning.

8:50 P.M. Bill bakes bread, while I stir a pot of macaroni and cheese. Daniel arrives with a rack of goat ribs, which he places over fire.

9:15 P.M. Two lions from distinct sides of the meadow begin roaring. Daniel appears, sits on rock next to fire, and finally says, "You must remember not to mention Nentikobe to any of these Masai except David. If you do, they may disappear back to Entaskera, and we will not be able to carry these things to the falls and down to Lake Natron. Please remember this. Also, since they will not accompany us when we four leave our base camps and look for the Nentikobe, only David and I will wash our spears here and in the falls. We will tell the other Masai when we leave them at camp that we must occasionally go off in the forest to photograph birds. You see, they know that there are many white people who look for birds."

August 22, Saturday, 4:00 A.M.

It is raining. A flannel shirt and two blankets keep me warm. Overtired and excited from the day, find sleep difficult.

6:00 A.M. Joe is awake. Hear Daniel talking near big tree. Men are about, now outside of tent making our fire. Joe unzips tent flap, sticks his head out, and says it is foggy. A turaco calls.

7:51 A.M. Feel strangely weak. Can't be sick. Have to make it to the falls. Go for water. Fish dart about in the bubbling hot spring. They have no fear of man. Nibble at my fingers. When I bring Bill's bread pan to scour with sand, they leap about inside of it, frenziedly eating the particles of loosened dough. Walking back to the tent, two collared ravens light on ground ten feet away. As I reach the tent, hear the call of Hadada ibis. Left and high above the green fringe of forest, through the fog, five ibis appear, crying, circle and fly off in the direction of Forest of the Lost Children.

8:30 A.M. Ready to leave. Feel so weak. Can I make it? I have to.

9:23 A.M. Now in the forest. Bill turns to ask me, "Have you ever seen anything as beautiful?"

"I haven't." Orange flowers along the way David tells us are called Olosida, mauve ones Osupkiai.

9:37 A.M. Daniel raises hand, signaling halt. Points spear toward greenness of small valley. An orange spot. Through the binoculars it becomes a bushbuck.

9:45 A.M. Find fresh lion and elephant signs on animal trail that we follow. Sometimes Daniel does not seem exactly sure of path. Several days ago when we met and I asked him how much time had passed since he has been to the falls, he replied, "A very short time." Now when we stop to rest and I again question him, he replies, "When I was a morani." Which was probably eight or ten years ago, if not longer.

10:00 A.M. Hear buffalo crash through reeds in front of us. Forest so tangled, some buffalo tunnels almost black inside. Crawl through them shouting and clapping hands. Arrive at small river and follow bank. Turacos' brilliant glide reflected in water. Hippo submerges in a pool in front of us. While resting, porters take snuff from small containers and sniff it into noses.

10:36 A.M. Daniel slashes trees along the way with semi knife. Don't question if this will help him find our way back in several days or if in the future when he returns with other white men, the way to falls will be better marked. Puzzled that with the thousands of immense tree trunks we pass, not one is slashed with horn of a unicorn; marks frequently found on trees in other parts of the world.

11:23 A.M. Reach edge of escarpment. Below lie miles of forest stretching out to four pale red peaks. And beyond the peaks, far to our right, can barely be seen the shimmering grayness of Lake Natron. Leave two porters here with backpacks.

11:45 A.M. Can hear falls in distance. Mountain down is so steep that one must grab saplings every step of way, using trunks almost as a skier poles down a slope. Through an open space in the trees. The falls! First view. White water cascading between curtains of forest. In that water Daniel will wash his spear in final Masai ceremony for approaching Nentikobe.

12:15 P.M. Reach falls. Lily clusters frame mossy banks of pool into which water plunges. David and one of the younger Masai climb carefully ahead with me, over slippery boulders toward pool. Soon wet with mist. Have we arrived at end of world—or is this the beginning of it? Weakness that I felt early this morning has completely left body. Tired after long climb, but exhilarated by everything can see, smell, touch, and hear. Gather and press wildflowers.

12:30 P.M. While Bill, Joe, and other porters have lunch, I return to base of falls with David and Daniel, who stick their spear blades into the pool of clear water. Daniel repeats a phrase in Masai several times. Remove dripping blades, hold them high to the sun. Again Daniel says something in Masai, this time only one word. Again the spear blades are plunged back into the pool, over which glide pair of pied kingfishers, crying sharply, "keek, keek."

1:46 P.M. While Joe and Bill take photographs and the Masai stretch out on grass, resting, I lean back on slick gray boulder that could be the back of a hippopotamus, bottom part of it wet and dark from the rushing run-off of the falls. Feel insides open up to release every bit of pressure, every bit of anxiety, every bit of worry that my life would never be fulfilled. All of those dark feelings are replaced by peace, a peace so great that I don't know or can't feel where I physically end and where the rock and forest and falls and sky begin.

2:00 P.M. Moving away from falls. Keep glancing back. Now must look forward as we start up hill.

2:35 P.M. Halfway along mountain, which seems practically straight up. The only way we can advance is to step by step grab onto saplings and creepers and pull ourselves forward. Porters complain that loads are too heavy. Daniel stops and hoists one of the backpacks onto his own tired shoulders, and Joe takes another. Grabbing on to vines for support, I think of snakes. Daniel says forest crawls with mambas, spitting cobras, and

Hippo

Leopard

Cape buffalo

Rhino

boomslings. But until now only trace was piece of dry skin at Oloololo Escarpment.

3:10 P.M. Reach outcrop where other porters and supplies were left. Light has changed on four red peaks in distance. Daniel says we will follow the edge of the escarpment southward, slowly working our way down toward Lake Natron, which sparkles distantly. As porters start to walk, Daniel calls me aside. "If we have very good luck, I know of a place at the edge of this escarpment which is not far from Lake Natron, and from which you will see Ol Doinyo Lengai, and there in a very dense part of the forest lives a Nentikobe with eyes the color of the sky. And when I have seen this animal, it had some flowers in the hair around its face the way you have described it to me." Why, I wonder, had not Daniel told me of this yesterday or the day before? Perhaps it is part of the pattern, piece fitting into piece, each at its own proper moment.

4:26 P.M., bottom of Nguruman Escarpment
Temperature changes as descend into Rift Valley.

The heat of the valley rose to meet us. Singing cicadas, butterflies like flowers before a wind fluttered against our bodies or hovered over the low bush. Only small things that were safe in the daylight moved. —Beryl Markham

4:45 P.M. We have followed, wherever possible, grassy corridors along the edge of escarpment, sometimes having to enter and again pass through heavy forest through which only way to proceed is to follow buffalo tunnels. Once Bill turns to me, removes his glasses, wipes the sweat from his forehead, and says, "I cannot believe this. This must make three hundred of these tunnels that I've walked or crawled through, and we haven't met up with one buffalo. I just don't know what we'd do, except probably die, if we did. You're sure that oil isn't good for them, too?"

"I wish it were," I answer, often now almost too tired to listen for buffalo in the high grass or as we enter a tunnel. "I'm going to tell Daniel to slow down. We're going too fast. You can't see anything this way. We have to go half this fast." Pushing ourselves too hard. Unhealthy when senses are numbed by fatigue. Diminishes sense of danger around us. Of party of nine, am the only one who would not be victim of lion or elephant attack; but am defenseless as are the others against Cape buffalo. Under heavy loads, Masai obviously less alert than they were this morning.;

5:05 P.M. Reach meadow at the edge of forest with high red rocks on one side and beginning of a marsh at far end. Unload packs, Bill and Joe begin setting up tent, and Masai establish their own camp and look for firewood. Light starting to fade. I call Joe, Bill, and Daniel aside and suggest that, tired as we are, we walk across meadow and along the marsh. Joe and Bill should follow well behind and to the right with their cameras. Now that Daniel's spear has been cleansed, am anxious for him to accompany me. Must take time out and forget forced-march mode; creatures of the forest have seen us—we have been making too much noise and going too fast to see them.

5:23 P.M. Now over quarter of mile from camp, follow clearing interspersed with clumps of brush. Reedy marsh one hundred yards to right. Look over shoulder. Joe and Bill remain practically out of sight behind us.

5:25 P.M. Cry of Hadada ibis. Daniel stops next to me and slowly places spear in ground. Movement in vegetation one hundred feet to our right. Flash of white through branches. Out of corner of eye see Daniel's mouth tense. "Nentikobe," he says softly, eyes fixed on bushes. Silence.

Slowly raise hands to mouth. Can see notes of tonal range on page of Springer's journal. Take deep breath and give low unicorn call-up sound. Everything still. Daniel stands like ebony statue. World seems to have stopped.

Slowly it appears, stepping delicately out from behind bushes. How can it move so quietly? Not even a twig snaps. First thing I notice are blue eyes. Old stag, at least five hundred years, maybe older. "Nentikobe!" I say, and a wide smile breaks across face as, unable to contain the joy that surges underneath my khaki shirt, I glance at Daniel. "Nentikobe!"

Unicorn stares toward us—but not at us—over, behind, somewhere possibly to where its horn sonar has detected the porters setting up camp, more than a half mile away.

Prepare to use second means of communication that Springer said would bring East African unicorns to within inches of human observer.

Suddenly, stag looks away from us and to the left. Hadada ibis cries from direction of marsh where unicorn is staring. "Simba!" says Daniel

Unicorn

Lion

Hartbeest

Elephant

quietly, as a black-maned lion emerges from the reeds and walks along edge of water, obviously not aware of the Nentikobe. Lion stands at water's edge for several seconds, staring at own reflection. Unicorn's eyes widen.

5:29 P.M. Lion slowly walks along edge of water. Forest lion appears stockier, fuller, and in better condition than even Masai Mara lions that were surrounded by prey. Lion changes course and starts to cross mud that extends into water. Glance at Daniel, who raises eyebrows in puzzlement.

5:30 P.M. Suddenly, lion glances up, yellow eyes fixed on unicorn. Hadada ibis calls again. Unicorn then rears high into air, mane cascading out in the breeze, tucks forelegs, strikes with hooves in direction of lion, then lunges forward and is off running through tall grass and brush in the direction of marsh. Lion snarls and bounds off behind reeds. I step forward to follow. Daniel grabs my arm, "It is alright with the Nentikobe for us to be as close as we were, but you cannot do that with a lion."

"Trust me." I pull away from Daniel. "You stay here. Wait for me here." I run toward tall reeds.

5:33 P.M. Can hear snarling and unicorn vocalizations somewhere ahead. Fortunately, Daniel has remained behind.

Then they are in sight. Raise camera, press release, nothing happens, look at film counter: 24. Loaded a 24-exposure roll instead of 36-exposure roll.

Unicorn rearing. Lion raises up on hind legs to full height, snarling, teeth gleam white in going light. Appear like boxers sparring, lion striking out with paws, unicorn with his hooves. Move closer. Stop. Then advance to within sixty feet of animals. Can see lion is not unsheathing claws as he strikes. All sounds and violent movements are of battle, but realize it must instead be part of some strange inoffensive ritual. Neither seems bent on wounding the other. Dropping to the ground, simultaneously and for several seconds with heads not more than a foot apart (the unicorn having lowered his horn with neck extended), stare into each other's eyes like mongoose and cobra. Ever so slowly, unicorn advances within an inch of lion's muzzle. Then the stag starts inhaling and exhaling furiously, something I had frequently observed wild horses doing in the Camargue in contests of dominance.

Suddenly, at same instant, lion roars and stag bellows. They separate, turn backs on one another.

Lion springs up bank and into heavy brush while the Nentikobe gallops along marsh to disappear behind a stand of acacia trees. In many years of unicorn study, this is first time have ever observed a stag or doe in close association with a large carnivore.

Return to Daniel, Joe, and Bill. When I tell what happened, Daniel says, "That is something not to be explained. Never have I seen the Nentikobe and Simba together, nor have I heard of it, not even in Masai legends." Shakes his head in puzzlement. "There are stories of Nentikobe fighting with the buffalo, which I have never seen, but I have heard about that."

"You got fabulous pictures then," Bill's eyes sparkle behind his glasses.

"Nothing," I answer looking down at the camera. "There was a roll of that twenty-four-exposure film that we bought at Keekorok. I thought it was a thirty-six exposure, and it was on twenty-four when I tried to fire it."

Bill starts to rewind his camera. "Well, I think I got a good one of the lion walking along the water."

"And I got one of you guys when the unicorn came out of the bushes, and when he ran away," says Joe.

"Fabulous," says Bill. Start back toward camp.

10:15 P.M., camp, edge of Nguruman Escarpment

A lion sounds as I pull blankets up around chin. Outside glows dying campfire. Have been in tent for almost one hour. Tomorrow we must start early and walk long if we are to get anywhere near Ol Doinyo Lengai. Can't sleep. Can't get unicorn and lion out of my head. Could a scene such as the one I saw today have been the basis, as Springer believed, for the unicorn-lion association on coats of arms and heraldry? Might some story or sketch of this violent but apparently nonaggressive ritual have reached the ear or eyes of someone, somewhere in Europe, where it was converted into a symbol of nobility and courage? The lion roars again, and I wonder where unicorn is just now.

August 23, Sunday, 7:05 A.M., edge of Nguruman Escarpment

Day breaks overcast. Have been on march for twenty minutes. Arrive at spot of unicorn-lion display. After porters have walked past site of confrontation, examine with Bill and Joe footprints in

august 22, edge of Nguruman Escarpment

moist earth. Tracks form a complete circle, to indicate that the ritual took place as I remembered having seen it. Daniel calls from ahead for us to move along. "We have a long hike," he says.

11:23 A.M. Arrive at manyatta. Stop to rest. Masai celebration.

Reported handsomeness of Masai not exaggerated.

A Masai warrior is a fine sight. Those young men have, to the utmost extent, that particular form of intelligence which we call *chic*;—daring, and wildly fantastical as they seem, they are still unswervingly true to their own nature, and to an immanent ideal. Their style is not an assumed manner, nor an imitation of a foreign perfection; it has grown from the inside, and is an expression of the race and its history, and their weapons and finery are as much part of their being as a stag's antlers.

The young Masai Morani live upon milk and blood; it is perhaps this diet that gives them their wonderful smoothness and silkiness of skin. Their faces, with the high cheek-bones and boldly swung jaw-bones, are sleek, without a line or groove in them, swollen; the dim unseeing eyes lie therein like two dark stones tightly fitted into a mosaic; altogether the young Morani have a likeness to mosaics. The muscles of their necks swell in particular sinister fashion, like the neck of the angry cobra, the male leopard or the fighting bull, and the thickness is so plainly an indication of virility that it stands for a declaration of war to all the world with the exception of the woman. The great contrast, or harmony, between these swollen smooth faces, full necks and broad rounded shoulders, and the surprising narrowness of their waist and hips, the leanness and spareness of the thigh and knee and the long, straight, sinewy leg give them the look of creatures trained through hard discipline to the height of rapaciousness, greed, and gluttony. —Karen Blixen

1:13 P.M. Manyatta—leaning against hut wall. Take notes and rearrange collected pressed flowers and butterflies in field guide. Joy in eyes of Masai children—the joy of all children. Here, however, "family," "friend," and "honor" are realities, not empty spoken sounds or meaningless words written on paper.

Is Masai fate similar to that of my countrymen? Will progress bring them the same "rewards"? A CBS report recently compared the seven major problems listed by American schools in 1940 to those in 1987. How innocent the concerns were of a mere forty years ago! Talking out of turn, chewing gum, making noise, running in halls, cutting in line, dress code infractions, and loitering. This has changed in 1987 to drug abuse, alcohol abuse, pregnancy, suicide, rape, robbery, and assault.

2:00 P.M., *edge of Nguruman Escarpment*
Again back on trail. Imagine Kenya was once heavily covered by forest like that which towers up around the path; like those being bulldozed under today, not only in Africa, but South America and Asia. That which is pure and beautiful—the natural world—is rapidly going the way of the unicorn.

2:23 P.M. Sudden break in forest at edge of escarpment. Straight out is Lake Natron. And far, far off to the right now uncovered by a drift of cloud is the Mountain of God. Not Kilimanjaro, as Hemingway wrote, but Ol Doinyo Lengai. It was in this very region one hundred years ago that Rudolf O. Springer became the first known naturalist to have close encounters with unicorns, not middle to distant observations that have always been the result of my fieldwork. If there is one time and place that I will stand close enough to a unicorn to feel its breath, it will be now and here. Daniel points ahead with his spear and says, "Ol Doinyo Lengai." Bill, Joe, the Masai, and I stand in silent awe of the Ngai, Ngai—the Mountain of God.

3:57 P.M., *camp, edge of Nguruman Escarpment*
Have set up camp at forest's edge. Five Masai and Daniel gone off to a nearby manyatta where they have friends, somewhere down toward Lake Natron. Say they will be back by nightfall. Bill is cleaning cameras and labeling film canisters. Ask Joe if he wants to go for a short walk. Picks up camera with long lens and joins me.

4:15 P.M. Promised Daniel that, unarmed, will not venture far from camp. Fisher's turaco calls from trees overhead. Now and then a flash of black and white, the long hair of Colobus monkey. This is second instance since we have been in the forest that have had time to leave behind the noise and movement of the safari. To forget the worry that the porters may drop backpacks and leave us if they see the Nentikobe. Realize that as long as Joe is close by, since he neither wears body oil nor is aware of other steps of Springer's formula, that close contact will be impossible.

4:28 P.M. Conceal myself on overhang that commands view of forest. Several hundred feet off to side and below, Joe is hidden in vegetation. Wait. Wait. Wonderfulness that comes with studying nature. Waiting. Observing the unexpected. Butterflies. Birds. Sounds. Fragrances.

4:45 P.M. Baboons bark far off, hidden below the canopy of trees that from this vantage point appear like immense expanses of broccoli clusters. Tropical bulbul begins its pump song. Swing the lens slowly to the left. Black sparkle among soft, lime-green blur of out-of-focus leaves takes form. White hair around black eye looking at me. Has been watching. Perhaps, since I arrived and stretched out to presumptuously feel that I was the viewer, not the viewed. Through leaves over the eye, above long white hair, it spikes through lush foliage. The horn. Not totallly visible, but enough to show spirals, between leaves.

Unicorn is staring at me. Should I try to call it up? Is Joe too close? Then there is a sharp whistle from right and below. Not a bird whistle, but a human one. And slight as it is, unicorn's eyelids flare. "Robert," comes Joe's voice from his hiding place. "Robert, do you see anything?"

At sound, unicorn bounds through the forest—in Joe's direction. Does it mean him harm? Never has there been a recorded account of an unprovoked unicorn attack in the wild. Is the Nentikobe of the Forest of the Lost Children different? Is there truth to the Masai legend of its dangerousness?

Unicorn leaps through vegetation, leaf patterns of sun and shade playing like water on silvery back. Now sounds the motor drive of Joe's camera, and the animal changes course to plunge into shadows, flashing mane like a wake of silver left behind in darkness.

5:55 P.M. Light starting to go rapidly. Follow heart-shaped familiar tracks to edge of a marsh. They disappear into water. Concealed in high reeds, I wait with Joe, who apologizes again and again for having spoken to frighten the Nentikobe. I tell him it is a young animal as revealed from very dark eyes. Quite similar to the unicorn, watched from Elm Tree, displaying on the shelf of red rock near Daniel's manyatta.

6:08 P.M. Legs are starting to go to sleep in this crouching position. Mosquito alights on Joe's neck,

I brush it away, and just as I have finished whispering, "Did you take your chloroquine this morning?" there is sound of swimming animal. Raise head, millimeter by millimeter.

Water is shimmering out, circling in flashing waves from the neck of Nentikobe as it swims toward shore, toward us. Toward the very place from which it had entered water. A lovely young doe whose delicate beauty belongs in a fairy tale. Now has gained footing, walking slowly out of chest-high then knee-high water, almost straight in our direction. Now, on land, stepping through tall reeds, which lash her silvery sides black with zebra stripes. Angles off to left and in seconds has disappeared into marsh. Joe does not speak a word as we get to our feet, his sparkling eyes say everything. Knees practically buckle with numbness, no feeling in feet at all.

8:00 P.M., camp, edge of Nguruman Escarpment

Daniel and Masai arrive after dark and gather wood for fire. They are in a good mood, after returning from manyatta where they visited with friends and drank pombe.

9:15 P.M. Daniel sits at our fire. "We saw a different Nentikobe today," I tell him about the unicorn.

"That is fine," he smiles, pulling the red and yellow blanket around his shoulders. "But I do not know if you are going to be able to be as close to this animal as you say you want to be. Many men see him, Masai see him, but none except the Laibons are allowed close to him, and even they may not touch him."

"But, Daniel, I've done it with elephants and lions. Why not with the Nentikobe?"

"Robert, you are a good man. But perhaps you drank pombe like we did today, and you think you were very close to those animals. Not even a Masai can walk up to those animals and escape with his life. Perhaps, it is true but . . ." He smiles.

"Have the people at the manyatta where you were today seen the Nentikobe?" asks Bill, eyeglasses ablaze with the reflected firelight.

"Those people, they see him. But you must not talk to them about that animal when we go to the manyatta tomorrow. It is a very magical animal, and there are very few Masai except the Laibons who do not fear it. Close to Ol Doinyo Lengai, you will see more of these animals. We will go to the manyatta tomorrow in the morning. They are having a celebration that you may want to photograph. Then we will go along toward Lengai, but we will keep near the forest for that is where this animal lives. Kwaheri." Daniel slips into the darkness toward the blaze of fire around which the porters sit singing.

11:15 P.M. Masai chanting softly around their fire. African wood owl hoots, "hoo-hoo, hoo-hoo, hoo, hoo, hoo." Jackals keen, and in the far distance, barely discernible, the call of a lion. We could turn back now, I think. We have found the Africa that sings outside this tent. We have seen three unicorns. Admittedly, we have not had time to study any one of them for periods long enough to make detailed behavioral notes, nor have I had the opportunity to call one right up to me. But we have seen them and know that they still actually exist here and not only in Springer's faded journal. Today is Sunday, August 23. We have tomorrow, Monday, the twenty-fourth, and Tuesday the twenty-fifth. On Wednesday the twenty-sixth we must start for Entaskera, which, doing a two-day forced march, we should reach on Thursday evening, August 27. Spend the twenty-eighth at Daniel's manyatta. Nairobi the twenty-ninth and thirtieth and leave for Spain on Monday the thirty-first.

Masai sing me to sleep.

They sang in voices that were so much a part of Africa, so quick to blend with the night and the tranquil veldt and labyrinths of forest that made their background, that the music seemed without sound. It was like voice upon another voice, each of the same timbre. —Beryl Markham

Monday, August 24, 10:45 A.M., manyatta, Kenya-Tanzania border
Arrive at a manyatta. Another Masai celebration. I sit in midst of decorated, chanting, exotically handsome people around whom spreads the most exotic of landscapes inhabited by the most exotic of creatures. Who but a fool would be surprised to find unicorns among these indigenous beings? Blue *salamis* butterfly almost lights on my knee.

Daniel and the porters disappear into crowd. "We better move on before Daniel and the others get too involved with this," says Bill, pointing to some Masai drinking beer out of gourds, "or we may be here the rest of the day."

11:05 A.M. Call Daniel and tell him to organize men, say we would like to stay but we still have a long way to travel.

12:15 A.M., Kenya-Tanzania border
Bill, Joe, and four of the porters are far ahead, almost out of sight, when Daniel, who has trailed behind with me and another Masai, stops, raises his hand, points to the right, and whispers, "Nentikobe!"

Running along a dark streamed at edge of the forest, a stag unicorn stretches out in full gallop. Masai porter next to me whispers, "Nentikobe. Nentikobe."

In a second, the unicorn, which appears much more mature than the animal seen the day before, is gone. Apprehensively, the porter looks at place animal disappeared as Daniel touches him on the shoulder and, speaking in Masai, points his spear at grass bent down in front of us by the porters' feet. Daniel then looks at me and softly says, "It is best that you give me twenty shillings to give to this man. He will say nothing." I unbutton one of the side pockets in khakis and pass Daniel the money.

"Nentikobe," repeats the man again, takes the money, and we continue, walking rapidly to catch up with Joe, Bill, and the porters.

2:15 P.M. In the distance a pink cloud drifts over blue lake. Lake is blue or is it pink? Colors merge. Flamingos, like petals from all the rose gardens of all the world, drift above water or on slim stems, blossom up from it.

3:15 P.M. Bill and Joe caught in the excitement of photographing birds. Finally, Daniel pulls up his spear and approaches. "You will have to tell your friends that we must continue if we are to arrive back at the forest where we will leave them, if there is still light, so that you and I can look for the Nentikobe."

4:50 P.M. Daniel, David, Joe, and I have left camp and are into thick forest. Bill with two porters has gone back to nearest manyatta to photograph bloodletting of cattle. Now the pace is slow. Stop to listen. Stop to look. The light on a leaf. Spiderweb tensing silver in breeze. Bird calls like organ notes in a cathedral echo and drift under green canopy. Take a few steps. Stop. Stop with time in truly virgin forest.

5:03 P.M. David, who has wandered off to one side, calls to Daniel in Masai. Follow his voice to

where he stands, looking at a strand of typical gray-green moss drifting with breeze. Into the moss have been woven brightly colored blossoms, the most prominent of which is *Notonia abyssinica,* a hairless herb with ascending stems and oblanceolate to obovate leaves. This is only evidence of bird-woven floral designs that we have found in Africa. Readers of *Unicorns I Have Known* will remember that in other parts of the world floral designs were often woven by resident birds into manes and tails of unicorns.

5:05 P.M. Joe signals with a low whistle. Daniel and I find him off to the left of the trail. Smiles at our approach and points to a pennant of green moss into which have been woven blossoms. Again, the predominant flower is *Notonia abyssinica.* But why are the birds weaving designs in moss and not in long hair of unicorns? I ask Daniel if he has ever seen flower designs in the mane hair of the Nentikobe. "No," he replies, "not like this in a pattern. But I have seen flowers sometimes in their hair around here." And he waves his hand around his own head.

5:12 P.M. Light starting to dim. Position ourselves fifty feet apart in forest. Daniel and I together. Joe and David together. Decide that in the hour before darkness takes form and color from forest, chances of seeing the Nentikobe are better if we wait for him instead of most certainly startling him by moving. Daniel and I stand at the edge of a clearing. Eyes strain. Ears strain. Strain to stand still. So still that breathing practically stops until only forest seems to be moving or sounding around us. Daniel appears, in his state of stillness, to have ceased to exist.

The civilized people have lost the aptitude of stillness, and must take lessons in silence from the wild before they are accepted by it. The art of moving gently, without suddenness, is the first to be studied by the hunter, and more so by the hunter with the camera. Hunters cannot have their own way, they must fall in with the wind, and the colours and smells of the landscape, and they must make the tempo of the ensemble their own. Sometimes it repeats a movement over and over again, and they must follow up with it. —Karen Blixen

5:22 P.M. Something! Movement forty yards away on far side of clearing. It steps out from behind the curtain of foliage. "Nentikobe," whispers Daniel and smiles. The unicorn now staring in our direction. Impossible, with his highly developed system of perception, that our presence escapes his awareness. Stag stands confidently in the magnificence of his maturity. Blue eyes indicate that he is at least five centuries old. Did Springer see this same animal, then perhaps dark-eyed, in the early 1880s? Green *Charaxes* butterfly flutters around horn.

Flowers. Now take notice of them. There is no intricate design, as studies have revealed in other parts of the world. Here in forelock, bluish purple blossoms are scattered as if by white water of cascade. Try to identify them. *Solanum `incanum? Clerodendrum myricoides? Pentanisia ouranogyne?* They appear more like *Ruellia patula.* First it seems they may have fallen onto and been caught up in the unicorn's forelock and mane hair as it ran through forest. No, sure to have been placed there by a bird. Curse myself at having allowed so little time for this expedition and for the study that should accompany it. Only four weeks, with the first two spent in national parks in preparation for the elephant and lion encounters that Springer adamantly instructed should precede meeting with unicorns.

If Daniel weren't with me or were farther away, would try to call up the stag, who is now feeding on tree leaves. Slowly raise camera and, once focused, fire off a frame, which is quickly followed by the sound of Joe's motor drive, somewhere off to the right. Nentikobe, at sound, rolls his eyes, tosses head, and begins to display much like that of the animal we observed from the top of Elm Tree near Daniel's manyatta.

"Be careful," warns Daniel, "that sound is not good to him." He glances down at my camera. "That animal can get very angry."

Unicorn now lifts his forefeet up in a half rear, similar to that of a carousel horse. Tempted to try and summon him to us with the call, yet Daniel's body is not protected with the oil. Only his spear has been cleansed with the hot spring and falls water. Also have vowed never to reveal second-step unicorn call—to anyone!

Unicorn's animation and display slowly escalate. Feel a tinge of apprehension. Never have been so close—close enough to see the blossoms shaken from mane and forelock hair—to a stag caught up in such dramatic display.

Leaps to right, literally diving into the brush, only to turn around and again face us. To see if we have fled? If we try to follow? What can be the purpose of retreating only to advance again?

"Be careful," whispers Daniel apprehensively, a slight tremor to his voice.

The stag is now rolling eyes to such an extent that in the going light they flash like aquamarine on a moonlit field of snow. Can it be that the odor of body oil mixed with acrid smell of Masai is confusing the animal? He wishes to approach, even though I have not called to him. Yet Daniel's smell and presence ward him off.

Something must be done, his excitement is boiling to point of no control. Slowly raise hands to mouth, cover mouth and nose with palms. Draw air up to rasp through throat and exhale out of nose. Follow rhythm and tonal description prescribed by Springer. Hearing unicorn warning signal, stag rears slightly, rocks back, and then, like a white-maned dolphin, plunges not more than six feet from Daniel, leaving emerald wake strewn with bluish-purple blossoms.

5:28 P.M. Glance at watch. Six minutes have passed, seem like six hours since the Nentikobe appeared and disappeared into the forest. "That animal had me worried," says Daniel, jabbing his spear handle into the ground.

"I can't believe it," says Joe, emerging from his hiding place and running toward us. Behind him is David, his fine lips stretched wide in smile.

"David," I say as they reach us, "weren't you afraid?"

"Me?" he grins. "A Masai afraid?"

"But I thought even the Masai were afraid of the Nentikobe."

"I was afraid when I was a very little, little boy," he smiles. "They tell us those things as children to keep us from going into the forest where we might become distracted playing games and lose our father's goats or cattle. But I have seen the Nentikobe many, many times. Sometimes very close. However, never so close as today and never dancing around and making those faces. And there is only one time before this animal that I have seen it with blue eyes."

"Oh, Joe," I say, "how can we leave here the day after tomorrow? These animals are very unlike any of the others. We've made only sightings. I don't have one real note on behavior."

Joe smiles. "Don't get greedy. You came here looking for Hemingway's unicorn and found one made of snow. Then you found the real thing,

something no one has seen, no white person, since Rudolf Springer. You came here thinking that Africa was a vanished species, and you found it." He casts his eyes up at the feather canopy fringed with gold of the setting sun. A Colobus monkey starts to hoot. "You can always come back. The important thing is to know that unicorns are still here and that Africa is still here—and that you are still here."

"What do you mean that I'm still here?" I ask.

"Well, that oil did work. If it hadn't, you could have been killed by an elephant or a lion. And when you think that it doesn't work with buffalo after all the buffalo trails we've been down and tunnels we've crawled through. That's worth celebrating in itself, though we're not out of here yet."

I do not say it, but I think it as we turn to go: "Being greedy is no good, but, oh, how I want to call up just one Nentikobe, close enough so that I can feel its breath on my face.

6:24 P.M., camp between Nguruman Escarpment and Ol Doinyo Lengai

Back in camp. Joe starts fire with wood gathered by Daniel. Forest from which we have come is now dark in shadow. A stag impala stands near hot spring, turns, and looks at me over shoulder. Horns twist in spirals certainly more exotic and unusual than that of the unicorn that we watched an hour ago in forest. Shadows like incoming tide sweep past our tent, across the clearing, and toward wave of green that rises up against dark sky. Soon all will be black except the creatures of our imaginations.

9:45 P.M. "Kee-oo," calls an African scops owl. The flicker of the fire through blue fabric of tent. Must be a rock under place upon which I lay. Turn over on side. Bill groans typically and says, "I should have gone with you today, but I didn't think you'd see anything. That makes, what? The fourth unicorn? And all I saw was them shoot that arrow into the cow's neck and collect the blood in a gourd. It was moving so much and the light was so dim, don't think I got anything at all."

"You have to use faster film," I say and roll over again.

"Well, tomorrow's the last day here. I'll go with you then." He sighs.

"Can't take anyone tomorrow." I feel sleep coming on. "I have to go by myself. Maybe Joe can be way behind with a long telephoto, but if I'm ever going to call up a unicorn and have a close encounter, it has to be tomorrow.

August 25, Tuesday, 10:26 A.M., somewhere between Nguruman Escarpment and Ol Doinyo Lengai

Daniel protested when Joe and I left camp at daybreak this morning. "You have no spears, no arrows, not even a knife," he said, pleading with his voice and his sad eyes as we departed. He will take Bill into forest in the opposite direction to photograph Colobus monkeys.

Joe and I walk slowly in the direction of Lengai. Grassland borders to left. Forest to right.

10:45 A.M. What shapes are those? Dark gray. Moving in the distance through the tall grass ahead and to left. Wildebeest? Reach for binoculars. Group of figures coming toward us. In focus. Masai. Hand binoculars to Joe. "They're morani," he says. "Like we saw near Embagai. Dressed the same. They've been through the circumcision ceremony and are now painted—decorated—leaving the meat camp where they've been living and are going back to the manyatta. The white paint around their eyes means death and rebirth of man. Daniel should be here, 'cause we're not going to be able to understand them."

11:06 A.M. Boys approach, smiling apprehensively. "Jambo," we say and shake hands. "Jambo. Jambo." Joe was right, if Daniel were only here. But why are they coming from the direction of Ol Doinyo Lengai? Ben Kipeno at Masai Mara had said that only elders, not morani, were allowed to go there near where the Laibons live. One of the youths wears, at the back of his head, a half halo made of sticks and ostrich feathers. Stands out from the group like a black angel. It is he who steps forward and says, "What are you doing here, looking for birds?"

"You speak very good English." I smile.

"Not very good," he answers. "I studied with the missionaries. So you are looking for birds. Big ones, like ostrich and bustard? Or small, like the ones who make their round nests in the trees?"

"We aren't looking for birds," I answer.

"Then you are looking for elephant or for lions? You know it is dangerous to be out here"—he gestures in a wide arc with his spear to the land around us—"without some kind of weapon. The buffalo is very bad, and there are many of them. Not so much when they are together, but there are old ones, very mean, that live in the forest."

There is an innocence to the boy's face, almost that of some noble creature from another planet. Yet we are the strangers from an artificial world who have invaded his natural world. Will he run or how will he react if I mention the Nentikobe? Today is our last day before turning back. What difference does it make? "We are looking for the Nentikobe."

"You are here looking for the Nentikobe," repeats the boy. "And you have seen it on your way here?"

"We have seen it four times," I answer. "But we have come here close to Ol Doinyo Lengai," I motion to the mountains far in the distance, "to try and find a very special Nentikobe. One who will not run, who has very blue eyes and hair like silver water."

"And you do not bring guns." The boy looks at our camera bags.

"No, we bring only our cameras," answers Joe, opening the bag so that the boy may see its contents.

"And why do you wish to see the Nentikobe?" asks the boy.

"So that these lands will always be protected and that men will never come here with guns to harm him."

"The Nentikobe is animal of magic. Among all of the animals he is like a Laibon. Do you know what a Laibon is?"

"Yes," I answer.

"Then you understand that the Nentikobe needs no protection. Would you wish that I take you and your friend to him? If you wish, we can go. But I must leave these morani here." He points to the other boys. "It would not be good to take them to that place."

"But it is alright for you to come with us to the Nentikobe?" I ask.

"Yes," answers the boy, the breeze shimmering the halo of feathers. "You see, my father is a Laibon there." He points his spear toward Ol Doinyo Lengai and then speaks to the morani, who turn and continue on their way. None protests, they do not even look back. "Now come with me," says the boy.

1:15 P.M. For almost an hour we have been walking due south toward Lengai, when the morani turns west and directs us into the forest. Once under canopy of green, he stops and says, "Have you been to the house of the Nentikobe?"

"I don't understand," I reply.

"The place where the Nentikobe lives," says the boy.

"You mean the forest?" I question.

"Yes, in the forest but where he has his house."

"No," I shake my head in puzzlement.

The boy glances up at sun through trees. "If we go there right now he may still be inside," he says. "When you have the time there of, let us say, four o'clock," he points to my watch. "After then it is difficult to find this animal in its house."

A red-bill hornbill calls continuously, "wot, wot, wot, wot, wot, wot, wot."

2:25 P.M. Into the forest. Deeper. Deeper. As we arrive at the bank of river of clear water, I begin to worry that there will not be time to find way back to camp.

The river . . . twisted down into the valley and gave life, in turn, to mimosa trees with crowns as broad as clouds, and long creepers and liana that strangled the sunlight and left the riverbank soothing and dark.

The earth on the bank was damp and pitted with footprints of the game that followed a web-work of thin trails to drink at dawn, leaving the racy smell of their droppings and their bodies in the air. The river forest was narrow and cool and vibrant with the songs of multi-coloured birds, and clotted with bright flowers that scorned the sun. —Beryl Markham

2:42 P.M. Reach edge of escarpment. "Now we are here," says the boy. "We must be very, very quiet."

"Where is it?" I question.

Boy points to a dark spot where a wall of earth rises up, practically covered by vegetation. "That is the Nentikobe's home. He lives inside of there. It is very dark inside of that place."

With binoculars, see entrance to cave. "Are you sure that he is inside of there now?" I ask.

"He is there," answers the boy. "Now we will go over here," he points to a spot where the forest is especially dense, "and we will wait until that animal leaves his house. Then you will see him, and if he does not see us, you may use those." He points at the camera bags.

Today is last day. Final chance to call up a unicorn. The last opportunity for a close encounter with a unicorn, using Springer's formula. Risked

198

August 25, somewhere between Nguruman Escarpment and Ol Doinyo Lengai

life with elephants and lion, and it worked. Can't leave without trying it with unicorn. "You go over there and wait with my friend," I say to the boy, pointing to hiding spot he indicated. "I am going up there, on that place, just above the Nentikobe's house."

"That could be very dangerous," says the boy. "Nobody has ever been so close to this animal. Not for many years. My father has said that there was only the man of hair of fire. Perhaps that was only a story told to him by his grandfather. He never saw it with his own eyes."

"I have the secret of that white Laibon with the fire hair." I smile at the boy. "I have his magic and the Nentikobe will not harm me. Now go, my friend, with this man to the hiding place and watch, and you will see that it is true."

3:08 P.M. Once Joe and Masai boy are concealed, invisible behind heavy vegetation, slowly start for the entrance to the cave, half circling it to left. Climb the hill fifty yards from the entrance. Climb above it and then cut across to a spot of earth a few feet above where the unicorn will appear if in truth he is inside and comes out.

3:30 P.M. Wait. Wait. Gray monkeys laugh from the top of large acacia next to cave entrance. Looking down to well-trampled earth that leads into the hole; sparkles of green shimmer when overhead leaves now and then part to allow last rays of the sun to slide through the forest. Beetles. Green metallic beetles that in other parts of the world were sure indications of the presence of unicorns. They crawl the soft-dirt cave entry, which is embossed with familiar heart-shaped footprints.

3:38 P.M. Half-cat, half-raven, the cry comes from far away. Then closer. Closer. The call of the Hadada ibis! Now the sound is above. Into the clearing a flash of metallic green, black, and purple feathers as the bird alights in trees below which Joe and the Masai boy wait out of sight. Bird turns its head in the direction of the cave to call once more, its long, red curved beak slightly opening and closing, near enough to be visible to me.

3:40 P.M. Worry after all of these days that Springer's oil will have dissipated and lost affect on my skin. Early this morning again wiped it into armpits and on feet. Silence. What is this long silence? Stillness broken not by a monkey, bird, or insect—only by beating of my own heart. Keep eyes on earth in front of cave entrance, which cannot be seen from here. Movement. Very slowly.

Pointed. Ivory-colored. Takes shape as more and more of horn comes into sight. The snow of forelock is barely visible through the brightly colored wings that cover it and the Nentikobe's mane. Resting on the white hair are dozens of butterflies in a still and seemingly dormant state. Some form patterns, not too unlike the avian floral designs. Within seconds, however, wings are moving. Can't identify them all: only *Cymothoe sangaris*, *Charaxes eupale*, *Salamis temora*, *Acraea*, and *Charaxes zoolina*. Then, in an instant, the air is petaled with color, and the butterflies are drifting off into the forest and gone. Only remain lifeless ones that are shaken from the Nentikobe's mane to the ground. Try to sit so still, yet remain relaxed. Springer emphasized that observer must remain relaxed. Oil alone is not enough.

3:43 P.M. Eye is so blue, sky blue. Wide open as unicorn surveys clearing below entrance to cave. Boot moves slightly to send a clod of earth rolling into cave entrance near animal's hind leg. Ears turn back in my direction. For certain was aware of my presence long before he emerged from cave, just as he knew that ibis was also waiting, but apparently I pose no more threat to him than does the bird. Hair on his back shimmers like the inside of a pale abalone shell.

3:45 P.M. The Nentikobe takes a step forward. What should I do? In moments he may be gone, lost in the forest. Have been fewer than ten feet away from him, but he ignores my presence. Must try the call, but he is too near. Must have a close encounter, but one in which he comes to me, not me to him.

Walking now. He is walking away. On path from cave toward forest. I stand up. Fifty feet separate us. Nentikobe continues walking slowly, never looking back. I take a step, then another, forward down slope after him. Stop. Will give him another fifty feet, keep one hundred feet between us. Now he enters deep forest. Over shoulder see Joe and Masai boy rise up out of vegetation. Indicate with my hand that they are to follow, but to maintain present distance from me.

4:12 P.M. Deep in forest, darkness coming early here. Nentikobe stops and begins browsing from acacias. Suddenly, there is a flash of green and purple as the Hadada ibis glides to perch in tree above the feeding unicorn. Now slightly more than two hundred feet separate us. A fallen tree marks halfway point. Slowly step forward. One step then another, keeping eyes on him and also on ground to avoid stumbling over creepers that twist across forest floor.

Arrive at fallen tree. Sit down on branch. Unicorn still feeding. Ibis preening wing feathers. Lean back on branch. Try to join its attitude. Look from Nentikobe to pen marking this notebook. Glance to right to see Joe and Masai boy take cover behind tree trunk.

4:23 P.M. Now is time. If not now, maybe never. Fix stare on unicorn's horn then shut eyes and project in mind, like transparencies in a slide show, Springer's formula. Step by step. Gestures. Rhythm of sounds. Order of sounds. Notes and pitch of sounds.

Open eyes. Stag has not changed position. Fan my lips out from face. Compress cheeks. Voice relatively high-pitched sound prescribed by Springer. Repeat call three times at four-second intervals.

As stag pulls head from branches, ripping off leaves that fan out green from mouth, he stares at me. Hadada ibis cries mournfully, flaps wings, and ruffles feathers in contentment.

Give second call. Five seconds pass. Repeat second call.

Then lean down lower against log, head directed at notebook, but watching out of corner of left eye.

Slowly unicorn begins walk toward me.

4:25 P.M. Nentikobe now twenty feet away. Continues walking closer. Closer. Closer. Closer. Now ten feet away. Blue eyes have shifted from me to beyond limb on which I rest. Attention is no longer with me. Closer. Now stops not more than two feet away, peering off into the trees with intense blue eyes. Difficult to follow Springer's instructions. "During close encounter with *Unicornuus africanus*, observer should avoid looking directly in animal's eyes."

Turn my head slightly. Let eyes glide up stag's legs, which seem to be shimmering in the darkness of forest. Up to chest, neck, and head, all the time keeping my head angled to give appearance that I am concentrating on pen and pad. Flowers, purple and blue, are scattered through forelock and around horn. Very few in mane. Forelock blossoms could perhaps have been part of a defined flower design before stag either shook head or rubbed it during sleep against the walls or floor of cave.

4:32 P.M. Stag seems so oblivious to my presence that ignoring Springer's instructions, caught up in the magic of a moment for which I have waited for almost thirty years, turn face so that now both eyes can focus on the white head that rises up so close to me that could almost reach up and touch it. No sooner has unicorn's face come into field of vision of both eyes than he turns head sharply down toward me, at the same time voicing a low growl. Pink muzzle so close that I can feel breath on my hair and face as I slowly turn eyes away from stag's and gaze straight ahead as he stares down at me. *Must follow Springer's instructions,* I think to myself, no matter of longing and temptations.

4:37 P.M. Finally, seemingly convinced that I am merely another part of the forest, stag lifts head, and as he does so, sighs, breath that has the fragrance of . . . of . . . what? Distinct and yet so difficult to describe. It is a mixture of freshly cut grass and breeze off tidal pools. Does that define it?

4:38 P.M. Hadada ibis catches my eye as it flaps iridescent wings and glides from tree. Comes straight on, then right angles off in front of us. Cries twice and disappears between immense tree pillars that support forest canopy.

4:39 P.M. Stag raises muzzle. Trumpets twice. Same call that Daniel and I heard the stag make instants before he displayed and charged off to confront black-maned lion at the far edge of the Nguruman Escarpment. Springer corroborates this by defining the call as one used by stag unicorns before confrontations.

Stag takes a deep breath, tenses, and without paying slightest attention to me, leaps over log inches from my face and in an iridiscent flash disappears into forest, seemingly guided by direction of the ibis's flight.

4:42 P.M. Joe is smiling as he approaches. The Masai boy, however, wears an expression of locked-in concentration. "You have not told me that you are a Laibon," says the boy. "Not even Masai Laibon place themselves so close to the Nentikobe. The magic you do made that animal blind to you. For him you did not exist."

"Oh, Robert," says Joe, putting his hand on my shoulder. "That was great. I never, ever thought we could get so close to one."

"I am not a Laibon," I say to the boy and take his hand in mine. "But I am your friend. If you had not brought us here today, I could never have approached that close to the Nentikobe."

"But you make his sound. You know how to speak his language." The boy is now smiling.

"But I cannot speak Masai," I answer, then look up at the gold-rimmed leaves overhead. "The sun will be down soon. We have a long way to go back to our camp. Can you take us toward the manyatta?"

"That is where I am going," answers the boy. "But a man who can speak with the Nentikobe must also see like the leopard in the night. I think that you do not need me."

"We will not find our way back without you," I say, realizing how wrong he is and how totally disoriented I am. Thinking of the unicorn, I say to Joe, "You heard him, he's sensed a lion near here and he's gone off to meet it."

"Robert," says Joe, "it's going to be dark in a very short time. Very quick. We have a long way to go. Don't be greedy."

"Come," says the morani, and we file off through the forest. Pause to collect dead butterflies that are scattered on earth at entrance to Nentikobe's cave. A Narina Trogon calls softly, "coo-coo," again and again.

7:10 P.M. In the blackness pace slows to half speed. Now at edge of grasslands. Frightened as crashing of a Cape buffalo erupts from somewhere ahead of our path. Even under light of dim half moon, the morani seems to be as assured and aware of the trail as he was with light of day. Several times when we stop, he says in a low voice, "It is not wise to walk about at night. Rhino. Elephant. Buffalo. Lion. Leopard can see us, but we do not see them until they are like this," and he holds his arms a yard apart. "We must be very careful."

Now, near the plains, sounds that were not heard in the jungle, chorus in the blackness. Hyena. Jackal. Nightjars. Anxious to see Bill, Daniel, and our campfire.

8:07 P.M. The morani stops, turns, and grins. "Do you smell it?"

Joe and I sniff in the night air, which to me carries no new odor.

"Do you not smell it? The man who speaks with the Nentikobe. It is your campfire. Do you not smell the smoke?"

8:24 P.M. "I was worried sick," says Bill as we round the tent to find him tossing a log onto the fire.

"Robert, where have you been?" Daniel's face is tense with concern as he continues, "It is very dangerous out there once we are in the night." He

then speaks in Masai to the morani, while Joe and I tell Bill of calling up the Nentikobe.

"I knew you should have let me go. Daniel and I spent the day chasing Colobus monkeys, and everytime I'd get my tripod set up and camera on it, I'd look through the lens and where they'd been seconds before there'd be nothing except leaves. Did it really come right up to you, like the elephant and lions?"

"If Joe's pictures come out, you'll see it. Oh, I'm tired," I sigh and sit down on ground next to the fire.

11:17 P.M. Too excited and exhausted to sleep. Bill and Joe breathing softly next to me have in slumber left Africa—who knows what images project in theaters of their dreams? What empty nights will seem those when the sounds outside—lion, hyena, jackal, a distant elephant trumpet—are no longer part of my experience.

August 26, Wednesday, 11:55 A.M.

Pace is hard and fast. Have reached edge of escarpment near four red peaks. Cut straight up now through forest. Tonight will camp at hot springs near Laibon's tree. Same camp used on Friday, August 21.

1:52 P.M., Lookout Point, edge of Nguruman Escarpment

Stop for lunch at lookout peak. Gaze back in direction we have just come. Where Lake Natron and Ol Doinyo Lengai should be, there is a wall of gray haze.

"Robert," says Daniel, leaving the porters to stand next to me. "There is something . . . if I could speak with you for a moment." We walk twenty feet into forest. "Is something wrong?" I ask. (Porters have complained all morning that their loads are too heavy.)

"No," answers Daniel. "There is no problem. It is that I wanted to ask you. That boy. The morani who brought you to the camp last night. He told me about the Nentikobe. He told me that you and the Nentikobe were together. I know that boy's father. He is a Laibon near Doinyo Lengai. That boy I am sure tells the truth. Did you sit with the Nentikobe?"

Is it that Daniel's eyes are sad, or is he merely of serious manner? "We did see the Nentikobe, and what the morani told you is the truth."

203

"Oh," says Daniel. "Then you are one with this animal," he states, as if it were fact.

"Is there anything wrong with that?" Daniel's somberness makes me anxious.

"No, the Nentikobe is a very magical animal. But then you are the enemy of his enemies."

"But I thought he had no enemies but man. Bad men. Even the lion is not his enemy." And then I remember Springer's journal. "You mean the buffalo. But we have passed hundreds of buffalo, and we have hardly seen one close. They've all run except the one at the manyatta on the other side of the hot springs."

"No, no, there is no problem." Daniel looks up from the ground at me. "We must finish eating and be on so that we reach the hot springs before night is there."

"Ko, ko, ko," trills a white-eared barbet.

4:23 P.M., Forest of the Lost Children

Rest in clearing. Fragrances of forest too many to savor. It is cool. Masai argue about who will carry packs. In a few days, at my ranch in Spain, Africa will be a dream, a part of past. The reality of now is sun on my face, pen between these fingers, the voices of the Masai even in argument are soft. A Colobus monkey hoots.

5:16 P.M., hot spring

We arrive! Behind is the Forest of the Lost Children, the falls, unicorn and lion, the escarpment, Lake Natron, Ol Doinyo Lengai, and a series of unicorn encounters that never would I have imagined possible. Masai have moved to the large tree above the clearing while we raise the tent.

5:30 P.M. Bill and Joe gone to bathe in the hot spring. First bath in five days. I stretch out on grass with this pen and pad of paper in fingers.

5:40 P.M. Returning from bathing, Bill and Joe tell me how wonderful water feels. Have promised myself not to step again into African water unless life depends on it. Bilharziasis. Things have gone too well. Remember. Bilharziasis. Am tired. Sticky with oil and sweat after the six days of safari. Tired but euphoric. "Go ahead," urges Bill, as he dries himself with dusty, stained towel. "The water's clear. It's hot. It's moving water. There aren't any snails there. All over Africa, it's the first time I've ever bathed in a stream, river, or pond."

"Come on, Robert," says Joe, fresh and clean from the hot spring. "It's great."

5:55 P.M. Water, clear as glass, shimmers with going sun. Gold ripples spread out around my knees as I sit. Fish nibble at fingers and swish against my body. Quietly stare into the water. No sign of snails. No sound but the bubbling of the spring. Then deep in the forest a baboon barks. At the sound, turacos call. And far, far off, is it there or not? The faint cry of a Hadada ibis?

9:40 P.M. Can't sleep. Why take that bath? Can take a bath tomorrow night from the jerrican on Elm Tree. "Never ever put your big toe into any water in the wild in Africa. Bilharziasis. Bilharziasis," echo words again and again. Safari has been perfect. Why take edge off by worrying about bilharziasis? If hadn't spent ten minutes in water, would be sleeping instead of worrying at this moment. Then it starts, rough and low, up and down like someone sawing wood just across the clearing from tent. Without raising his head, Joe whispers, "Do you hear that? What's that?"

"A leopard," I answer and forget about snails and the devastating disease they carry.

10:26 P.M. Have just gotten . . . must have just fallen asleep, when there is movement next to me. Open eyes and see Joe's silhouette against the blueness of tent outside of which fire still blazes.

"Anything wrong?" I ask.

"I'm sick," he replies.

"Anything I can do?"

He unzips tent door flap, grabs a roll of toilet paper, and disappears. Poor Joe, can hear him retching outside. Unzip tent and stick head out, "Are you OK?"

"Awful," he answers from barely lit far side of fire.

"Don't get too far from the fire," I whisper, thinking of the leopard.

August 27, Thursday, 5:45 A.M., Hot Springs Camp

Joe has been sick, in and out of tent all night. Awaken to Masai singing. Am tired and mood is low, maybe with realization that the safari is over. Excitement is going. We are almost gone—back to other world. Hear Daniel making the fire. Joe and Bill sleep. In faint light Joe's bleached face and deep, dark circles under eyes, make me anxious.

5:50 A.M. Carefully unzip flap. Try not to awaken Bill and Joe. Amidst black thoughts surfaces the word bilharziasis. Day is gray. Walk down to hot springs and with a twig poke among underwater vegetation, but find no evidence of snails. Walk to boulders above spring and sit down. I am tired. Now that end is near perhaps am relaxing as adrenaline flow gives way to fatigue. Have to remember Joe's words about not being too greedy. Think about unicorn displays that we have seen, the call-up, and close encounter. Should spend the next six months here with time to do detailed behavioral study. Joe is right. If it had not been for Springer's journal, we might have come and left East Africa without ever seeing Nentikobe—most people do.

"Robert," comes David's low voice from behind me. "Robert." David is crouching down, looking toward hot spring fifty yards away. Cape buffalo stands where I had been looking for snails just minutes before. Head up, buffalo stares in our direction, snorts, turns, and runs off through high green grass to edge of the forest two hundred yards away. Once there, whirls and stares at us.

"He will return," comes Daniel's whisper from behind us. "I think this must be the bad buffalo they told us about in the manyatta where we bought the goat. You remember. Wait here. We will try to spear him. He will be back."

5:57 A.M. With David I wait concealed behind boulders. Daniel and two of the Masai have crept downstream into the tall reeds, and now wait out of sight with spears. Carefully I move head to side of boulder until I can see that buffalo is halfway in the middle of clearing, coming toward hot spring. Somehow, I hope he escapes. If the Masai only wound the buffalo, will they follow him up into the forest, or let him die there, suffering, and maybe killing someone while he waits.

Even though Springer had no great love for Cape buffalo (no one has whom I have met on this trip), and though his formula is not successful with them, still I do not wish to see this animal die, though he be the only enemy of the Nentikobe. What if buffalo wounds or kills one of the Masai? It is no good. Feel like standing and frightening him away as he now draws closer, carefully walking toward the pond. But this is Masai land. Theirs, not mine.

"Choo, choo—too—wee!" comes the loud, clear whistle of an emerald cuckoo.

And this morning is a soft, green morning when death, which never seems remote in Africa, but hangs about like something half-remembered, might

come almost companionably . . . be that as it may, I leave my doubts behind. —Peter Matthiessen

5:59 A.M. Buffalo now at the water's edge, peering directly at us. Suddenly voices behind. Bill and Joe, not aware of hunt. The buffalo turns and crashes off again, leaving an impression of bent reeds behind. Arrives at forest, turns, looks back at us, then disappears into trees. Relieved there is no hunt, but puzzled why buffalo with such keen perception would return in such a short time to place he had seen men.

"He was probably just thirsty," says Bill.

9:00 A.M. Joe now sick with chills and fever. Will break camp in an hour. David accompanies me into hills at the edge of Forest of Lost Children to gather and press wildflowers into bird field-guide book. David and Daniel, I feel I know, but not as they know me.

On our safaris . . . my acquaintance with the Natives developed into a settled and personal relationship. We were good friends. I reconciled myself to the fact that while I should never quite know or understand them, they knew me through and through, and were conscious of the decisions that I was going to take, before I was certain about them myself. —Karen Blixen

12:15 P.M., Loita Hills

Bill has stopped with group of Masai in front of me. Masai poke into grass with spears. Approach. "Look," he says, "they say that's a poisonous lizard. I want to photograph it." The spears press a common chameleon against the grass.

"It's only a common chameleon," I reply and start to walk on. "Come on!"

"But they say it's poisonous, and I want to photograph it," says Bill setting up his tripod. "Besides, everyone is too spread out. We should all stay closer together."

I walk on. Then realize that Bill has waited for me dozens of times, and has stayed in camp when he wanted to join Joe and me looking for the Nentikobe. If he wants to photograph a common chameleon that Masai superstitiously believe is poisonous, why not? I call to Daniel and tell him to shout ahead to the porters who have just arrived at the bog of black water. "Tell them to wait for us." Return to Bill and apologize.

12:30 P.M. Stand at edge of bog as Masai wade across and Bill and Joe take off shoes, socks, and trousers. "BILHARZIASIS" block letters flash somewhere in my mind. Again, this is a reality of Africa—a danger that could mean death, which has barely been visible to us in the Forest of the Lost Children.

Remove boots, socks, and pants and step into water. Sucking black mud oozes over ankles, and water swirls around knees, grab onto reeds to keep balance.

12:45 P.M., manyatta

Have stopped at manyatta where goat was purchased several days before. Children approach Daniel and each porter and reverently lower heads. Daniel and porters gently place hands on children's shaved heads. Joe says he is feeling very weak. Then Daniel and porters go inside of hut to drink milk and blood. Soon Daniel emerges from hut with low wooden stool, which we place in shade of tree for Joe. Bill jokes with and photographs group of Masai women and children.

Watching children, wonder at absence of fawn unicorns. Not one seen, nor signs of existence detected. Of five unicorn sightings: four stags and one doe. Springer reported having observed a more or less equal male-female ratio with numerous fawns also recorded.

1:07 P.M. Daniel and porters come out of hut. Help each other load backpacks. As we leave manyatta, one of the villagers shows us a black goat that had been attacked by a leopard.

1:10 P.M. Walk up grassy corridor toward finger of forest where six days earlier safari had been threatened by Cape buffalo. Masai behind us set fire to dry grass. Stop Daniel, who is walking ahead. "Why are they doing that?" I ask him.

Daniel turns, wiping the sweat from his brow, and replies, "You see, there are many cobras and mambas in this grass. Very bad snakes. They bite these people's cattle," he gestures toward the manyatta. "They rid this place of those bad snakes." He turns and continues up the hill.

1:17 P.M. As we move toward edge of forest, near the place of the buffalo challenge, Bill ambles toward trees.

"Come this way," Daniel warns. "Stay away from there. Come this way."

1:25 P.M. Walk around finger of forest that sticks out into grassy passageway that is several hundred feet wide. Look back over shoulder and see billows of smoke rolling up from fire set by the Masai. Ahead Daniel, leading, then Bill. Behind is Joe, followed by David and the four porters. *Shouldn't be so spread out*, think to myself. *Should be Masai in front as we had always agreed during the safari. Three of four Masai in front, followed by us and one or two porters behind.* But fatigue overcomes better judgment, and as with the bog and bilharziasis, step tiredly forward, thinking of the long hike ahead, and don't stop to reorganize the line of march.

1:30 P.M. Eyes on grass in front, concentrating on mambas and cobras, which Daniel says infest this place.

Then the crashing!

The fear!

My heart pounding. The bellow. Daniel's red and yellow blanket a blur as his arm coils back then forward to lance the spear. A black mass. Turn and run, run as I have never run in my life, to save my life. (What follows is the entry from Joe Saccoman's diary.)

Daniel, our Masai guide, was in the lead. Bill was second, Robert was third, I followed Robert, and trailing by twenty-five yards were five Masai with spears in hand, carrying our supplies.

The ground thundered, branches crashed, and there appeared a blur of black to our front right. The others ran for the forest on the far side of the grass corridor. It seemed shorter to me to run diagonally away from the bull, back to the same side of the forest from which he had charged. The Cape buffalo singled me out, and when I reached the edge of the forest, we were face to face, separated only by one small tree, with three wrist-sized branches spiraling upward—a tree too small to climb.

As he charged, I moved away, keeping the tree between us. He bellowed aggressively, matching me move for move as I tried to outmaneuver him, my eyes focused on his as I sidestepped back and forth then ran around the tree. My adrenaline was almost gone, I was exhausted. He stopped for a moment, and we stood there, looking at each other, our faces three feet apart.

I was dazed, wondering what I was doing in front of this devil. The voice of Kununga, who had been our guide on the safari to Olmoti and Embagai, came back to me:

"If you are on the ground, lie flat—very dangerous—if he gets you up, he will tear you apart with his horns."

Got to get away, I thought.

"Someone throw a spear!" screamed Bill from across the clearing.

The bull backed off two steps into the forest, and I dashed off toward the ghost of my friend's voice.

Halfway across the clearing, my legs tied up and I fell, face first, sliding on my palms. The bull ran over me, but he was too close to have time to lower his horns. He swept over me and circled back, but I had scrambled to my feet, fighting to gain speed. He came from behind again and hammered me forward five more yards. I landed on my feet running, but he hit me again. I tumbled about five yards, which left me sprawled fifteen feet from the tree in which my friends had taken refuge.

A split second after I stopped rolling, there was a pounding on my chest, then my whole body was slammed back. I saw a mass of black horn boss and huge brown-rimmed eyes a foot from mine as the buffalo tried to batter me into the ground. My senses blurred white, as—bellowing and grunting—he smashed me. A white flash of pain through my back. Each crushing blow whitewashed my senses with pain—and still he kept ramming me. Was he slicing me with his horns?

Only minutes had passed, but time slowed as my body went into shock, and it seemed that the buffalo had been on top of me forever. There was no way to get him off. Something warm was soaking me. I saw blood pouring everywhere, but in the storm of the attack, I couldn't tell if the blood was his or mine. How much longer could I survive? I thought that I heard a distant scream, then realized that it was my own voice—far away.

I relaxed, giving in to death as the buffalo thrashed me a few more times—then I was alone.

There was an instant of quiet, then I heard Robert shouting. Rolling my body to the left, I saw that Robert had jumped out of the tree and was advancing, frantically waving his arms and madly shouting to decoy the animal. It charged him and ran him around the tree twice. As the bull came around the second time, it stopped ten feet from me and stared, again looking into my eyes. Slowly I reached back to untangle my leg from a bush.

"Hold still—don't move," monotoned Robert, hardly moving his lips as he saw me reaching.

I slowly lay flat again, watching the Cape's wild eyes, hoping that he wouldn't charge.

Robert waved and yelled, and again the buffalo turned on him, chasing him around the trunk two more times, and while the buffalo was on the far side, a Masai, seated high up in the tree, threw a camera bag at it. The bull charged the bag.

"Run, Joe!" came Robert's voice, as Bill, from his perch, threw a sixty pound duffle bag onto the buffalo, which it tossed ten feet into the air as if the bag were a feather pillow.

With a surge of adrenaline, I freed my leg from the bush and lunged two steps to the tree. I climbed the trunk with Robert pushing and Bill pulling.

A nauseous feeling engulfed me. I collapsed against Robert, his arm around my chest, my head seven feet from the ground. I was covered with blood. I coughed and Robert told me to spit into his hand. The mucous was red.

Internal injuries or puncture wounds, I thought.

"A tremendous blackness lifted from me as I realized that Joe was alive," Bill later wrote in his diary, "however, I fully suspected that internal injuries would be fatal immediately . . . I knew that we had to kill the buffalo or we would be caught in this tree for days, and time was of the essence for Joe's chances of survival."

The bull came back to the tree and grunted, straining his giant eyes upward, but, unable to bend his thick neck, he couldn't see us. I was suddenly sick and threw up, spattering his horns.

In the top of our tree was a Masai warrior, then Bill, and below him, Robert, who kept me from falling.

There was a sudden pain in my back, and it hurt to sit up.

From his perch above, the Masai shook the top of a small tree, which the buffalo charged, then bellowing deeply next to us, the bull spun in the opposite direction. There he stood, statuelike, as if waiting for his next victim. I could see the deep lines of the tendons in his cheeks and brow that stretched his eyelids open.

"Do something, Daniel. Throw a spear—please do something!" yelled Bill. Daniel was hidden from sight behind us in some tall trees. "We've got a man dying up here—do something! Joe's dying!" pleaded Bill.

No reply.

The bull grunted again and turned his head to the base of our tree to slam his horns against the trunk, blood from his neck wound speckling our boots as he charged. I tried to pull myself higher into the tree. My back was buckling.

"I feel like I'm passing out—can you hold me up?" I asked Robert.

Robert's leg was completely numb by now. He pulled me up tighter, his eyes were filling with tears.

"We've got to build him a frame," said Bill, "before our strength runs out." He pointed to a limb beside the Masai. "That one," he commanded, making a chopping motion with his hand to the warrior.

They slid a series of limbs under me for support.

It must have been three o'clock, and an hour had passed when now the crackling sound of the grass fire moved in behind us. Smoke seeped through the forest, discoloring the sun spots on the leaves. I could see blood flowing from the buffalo's neck wound as he continued charging the small tree.

"You've got to help us!" yelled Bill in desperation.

"We don't have any spears left!" came Daniel's reply.

Two more branches were slid beneath me.

Twenty minutes later the buffalo walked ten yards away from us. The strongest of the Masai, under the cover of thick vegetation, came from behind and threw his retrieved spear in an unerring arc seventy-five feet, striking the bull high behind the shoulder and sinking the spear three feet into the animal's side.

"It wasn't low enough, Daniel! David, it wasn't low enough—you'll have to throw another spear!" shouted Bill.

"We don't have any more!" yelled David.

The bull walked thirty feet farther away, probably going away from the fire, which crackled ever louder.

"He's down!" yelled Bill. "There's a spear right below us."

"Do it now, David!" shouted Robert. "He's down!"

David stalked behind the bull and hamstrung him with his machete, then lodged the final killing spear in the bull's heart.

Six Masai lowered me down from the tree, the

Cape buffalo
August 27, Loita Hills

bend of my left arm pulling hard on Daniel's neck, as I tried to ease the pain in my back. They laid me down on a blanket in a clearing.

"We'll have to drive him to Nairobi," said Bill, as he pressed his fingers against my distorted spine, then pulled off my bloody shirt. "Can't call in the air pilots—sometimes take them twenty hours to deliver." He took off his glasses and rubbed his eyes, then put his glasses back on. "You can't imagine how hard I was praying in that tree!"

With five Masai, Bill left for the Land Rover in a run that would take him several hours.

Within twenty minutes I was out of shock. We agreed that we had never felt so alive as we did in those moments. "My God, man—Africa was never seen like this by Hemingway!" exclaimed Robert, enthusiastic now that I seemed to be recovering. "They always had white hunters with guns and carried guns themselves." He focused a camera for David. "When you tell somebody about this, tell them to multiply the drama and intensity by a hundred times. A movie was never made that could depict what we saw!" He walked behind me, and David took our picture.

Hours later, the nightmare continued. Even though I lay on my back in the security of the Land Rover, the light was fading and there was no immediate road to follow. We were desperate to find a shortcut out of the forest before it was totally dark. Robert and Daniel were running in front of us, trying to guide us to the dirt road, scouting for washes and warthog holes while watching out for lions and Cape buffalo. We turned back five times before finally finding the way out of the forest.

From there it was a bumpy eight-hour drive in the dark back to Nairobi, where my injury was diagnosed by Dr. Alberto Bencivenga as a compression fracture of the L1 vertebra.

As in William Blake's *The Marriage of Heaven and Hell*, there are two contraries to paradise, good and bad, tranquility and fury.

In the fury of the attack, we had been stripped of everything but our bare selves. In a primeval setting, we saw humankind as a fragile animal able to survive naked only by bravery, camaraderie, and quick thinking.

I realized a peace proportional to its opposite—fury. Living only in tranquility is being only half alive.

Africa has intensified my sense of childlike curiosity—that sense of wonder that makes life exciting. I learned how important it is to be in intimate contact with nature.

We counted ourselves lucky to have come so close to nature—so close to this most basic reality—and realized that all of our future experiences would be weighed against the impressions of this day.

I'm in a brace now, there's no nerve damage, and it will take another six months to determine whether or not back surgery is needed. I am now attending San Diego State University. —Joseph Saccoman

August 30, Sunday, 10:15 A.M., lobby of Norfolk Hotel, Nairobi

Bill and Joe left yesterday near midnight on Pan American flight. Nine seats removed to accommodate the stretcher. Nairobi, London, and Los Angeles, where an ambulance will be waiting to take Joe to San Diego. Joe is alive. Joe is not paralyzed. I am happy. I am alive and in Africa. I have not only seen but had a close encounter with the Nentikobe. With a herd of elephants. With a pride of lions. Who deserves such happiness? And most important, Joe is alive.

Lobby is a continual parade of tourists in acrylic safari suits, parading about like guests at a theme costume party. I wear a polo shirt, jeans, and white tennis shoes. No longer have to display and prove that I want to be part of Africa. Must be part—now.

12:30 P.M., Lord Delamare Restaurant, Nairobi

Lunch with Liz McGill. Tonight I will spend with Liz, her husband, and four-year-old son Doiky at their home in Karen. Return from changing money and to table for dessert. Have not mentioned the Nentikobe to Liz. For the past few days everyone's talk is of the buffalo. Before we leave the table, Liz leans across and says, "You know, I was thinking. You are a very brave man. And fast. Most people would have been in such shock that they couldn't have jumped down from that tree if they had wanted to."

"I don't know if you can call bravery something in which there was no choice," I reply. "Joe was going to be dead in seconds. What else could one do? You see, there really was no choice for me, and bravery indicates a choice."

"That's your way of seeing it," replies Liz. "But you did have a choice, and I heard you tell Bill that you thought you were going to die when you jumped down. But I won't argue with you over that. You do know that you've had the opportunity that few men ever live to enjoy."

"What's that?" I question as she smiles a lovely smile.

"You've been able to know the extent of your courage, that it has no limits," she replies.

3:25 P.M., Hardy House, Nairobi

I sit on the back steps of the McGills' house. In the garden, four-year-old Doiky plays with Mutua, a black boy perhaps twice his age. The garden is a fugue of finch songs—firefinch, cordon-bleu, waxbills, mannikins, cut-throats. Beyond garden is the forest above which rise the Ngong Hills.

"Robert," says Doiky as he approaches me, his eyes sparkling as blue and clear as his father's, "Robert, did you see a lion on safari! I saw one, you know."

"I saw a lion. And I saw zebra and elephant and buffalo."

"My mother told me about the buffalo. You are the first hero that I've met. She said you were one. But I've seen elephant and zebra."

"And I saw another animal," I pick a jasmine petal and put it to my nose. "I saw an animal called Nentikobe."

"I don't know that animal." Doiky's eyes question me, "I don't know that animal. What does it look like?"

"Well," I begin, "it looks like a zebra except it's white. It has no black stripes, and it has a horn that sticks straight out right here," I touch my forehead.

"Oh, him," smiles Doiky and looks over his shoulder at a large tree in the center of the garden. "I've seen him."

"In a book?" I ask. "In one of your story books, I bet."

"No," replies Doiky impatiently. "Right here. Out there by that tree. Sometimes he comes here at night. I hear his noise when everyone is very asleep. I go to the windows and look out, and he stands by that tree. He rubs it with his horn and then he goes back there." Doiky points toward the Ngong Hills. "Robert, do you want to eat some biscuits with us?"

"Not right now," I answer and leave the boys playing with sticks in the dirt as I cross the lawn to the large tree. Trunk of tree is unblemished except . . . except six feet up, on the side that faces the Ngong Hills, there is an almost horizontal slash, perhaps eight inches long with a hole jabbed above and beneath it, like a division mark. Impossible. But it is a unicorn marking. Have seen too many in other parts of the world, but never one quite like this. Impossible. How can it be that in the Loita Hills, the Forest of Lost Children all the way down to Lake Natron, and almost to Doinyo Lengai we saw thousands of trees and never one unicorn bark-marking? Perhaps it was simply that here in the garden, there is only one tree and that in the forest there were so many that in rush to arrive at places for unicorn sightings, I was as unobservant as had Bill and Joe been in Olmoti and Embagai. So there are unicorns—or at least one unicorn in the Ngong Hills. In the forest beyond the garden sings a cuckoo that we heard frequently in Forest of Lost Children but never saw.

In Africa there is a cuckoo which sings in the middle of the hot days in the midst of the forest, like the sonorous heartbeat of the world, I had never had the luck to see her, neither had anyone that I knew, for nobody could tell me how she looked. —Karen Blixen

11:12 P.M., Hardy House

Wake from dreamless sleep but with a thought that I want to be in Africa. Remember Hemingway's words: "All I wanted to do now was get back to Africa . . . had not left it, yet, but when I would wake in the night I would be listening, homesick for it already."

Uninvited moon enters window. House is still. Everyone asleep below on main floor. Carefully get out of bed and slowly find my way to door. Cool outside. Turn slowly to left and walk past cages of African gray parrots along balcony until I can see garden below and rising out of the garden, the tree. Strain eyes. Is there movement? A light shape in the shadows? Is there movement, or is it my imagination? Beyond the garden and forest, far off rise the four peaks of the Ngong Hills. I breathe in fragrance of night, so perfumed with flowers that it makes me heady, and listen to the sounds that, after the sun rises in the morning, who knows how long it will be before I hear them—again? "Kee-oo, kee-oo," comes the soft cry of the African scops owl.

August 31, Monday, 1:15 P.M., Karen Blixen's house

Sit in this house, which before was built of black words on a white page but now is sound, touch, and color in my mind. Liz has kindly brought me here where I wish to finish these journal notes of the 1987 Elm Tree Unicorn Expedition. Have not left Africa, but already I am missing it so. Sit in this room with the curtains blowing in breeze, and with its dark wooden panels and the rich smell from old, fine wood.

I used to sit and write in the dining-room . . . My houseboys asked me what I was doing; when I told them I was trying to write a book, they looked upon it as a last attempt to save the farm through the hard times, and took an interest in it. . . . They would come in, and stand for a long time watching the progress of it, and in the panelled room their heads were so much the colour of the panels, that at night it looked as if they were white robes only, keeping me company with their backs to the wall. —Karen Blixen

3:30 P.M. As the light moves, I move outside to sit and write at the millstone.

On the Western wall of my house there was a stone seat and in front of it a table made out of a mill-stone. . . . The mill-stone table in a way constituted the centre of the farm, for I used to sit behind it in all my dealings with the Natives. From the stone seat behind the mill-stone, I and Denys Finch-Hatton had one New Year seen the new moon and the planets of Venus and Jupiter all close together, in a group on the sky; it was such a radiant sight that you could hardly believe it to be real, and I have never seen it again. —Karen Blixen

The going light warms the foliage at the edge of the garden. Movement. I look up. A bushbuck appears, perhaps some distant relative of Lulu.

The Ngong Hills, and the surrounding country, were good places for bushbuck . . . in the early morning, or at sunset, you would see them come out of the bush into the glades, and as the rays of the sun fell upon them their coat shone red as copper. The male has a pair of delicately turned horns. —Karen Blixen

The bushbuck is as lovely a creature as one could hope to see. In its own way, as lovely as the Nentikobe. The difference being that the bushbuck is common, while the unicorn—pursued, hunted, and pushed toward extinction by man—is rare. But in its beauty the bushbuck is as rare. Man, unfortunately, judges value on quantity. If one has lots of money, that is of value. If one has one of many, that is not of value. If one has one of a very few, then that one has value. The bushbuck has as much value as does the unicorn, I think. Some might even find his coat richer, and his two delicately turned horns more decorative than the unicorn's single straight horn. And one day if there are as few bushbuck as there are unicorn, if man has destroyed them and their habitats until they are considered "rare," then to men in general they also will have great value. "Ki-waa," comes the harsh double warning note of a red-fronted barbet.

My eyes leave the copper bushbuck. Above the trees are the four peaks of the hills that "rise like immovable dark blue waves against the sky." That haunting phrase, "I had a farm in Africa," reminds me that all possessions, land or whatever they be, are borrowed for this one lifetime; and borrowing implies treating with respect that object which has been entrusted to us. Karen Blixen, Isak Dinesen, however you wish to call her, lies deep under cold ground off in some place called Denmark.

Eyes slide down from mountains onto treetops and darkening foliage. Bushbuck is gone. In a little more than seven hours, aboard an Olympic Airways flight, I will also be gone from here—yet not really gone.

September 30, Wednesday, 7:30 P.M., Cañada Grande, Spain

Now I sit in this familiar Spanish garden with these familiar African dogs. A month has passed since I left Africa. Had forgotten the loveliness of this place. I had forgotten how I feel for these animals. How they feel for me. I am back in this garden—that is, almost back.

Kilimanjaro, Amboseli, Masai Mara, Athi Plains, Ngong Hills, Oloololo Escarpment, Loita Hills, Forest of the Lost Children, Nguruman Escarpment, Natron, and Ol Doinyo Lengai: Each is a deeply rich tapestry that hangs, appears, and reappears, in the museum of my mind. Faces and figures move through, up, and behind those threads of woven memory. Daniel, Simon Makallah, Ben Kipeno,

Shadrack Ole Lensir, David, the morani with black halo, Doiky McGill, and Mutua, Joe, Bill, and the ghost faces behind the curtains at Karen Blixen's house. And there are the animals. The tusker rumbling in charge behind me to stand calmly, ivory gently brushing the white of my legs; there was the golden-maned lion stretched beside me somewhere on a place that distinguishes Kenya from Tanzania. There was the buffalo. For nights, I could not shut my eyes without seeing his flaring nostrils erupting in silver sprays of saliva. The great open eyes rimmed in tones of white, brown, and blue. The massive spread of horn, banging against the tree trunk in explosions of bark as he tried to smash, stamp, gore, and crush life out of the creatures that had invaded his forest. In those anxious awful moments in the tree, as I held Joe in my arms, his spine bulging out against my ribs, life seemingly going from him like strength from my legs that had been cramped into the tree trunk for more than an hour, I hated the buffalo and I hated Africa. But that hate lasted until the nightmare was over, it vanished with the torment and terror of a bad dream. No, I do not hate the buffalo. One can hate a man, though that is not wise, but to hate a beast such as the buffalo would be totally unreasonable. In the forest everything about the buffalo represents the forces of evil. I do not hate him, though his charge was unprovoked. He made a choice in his animal mind and died because of it, and almost killed Joe doing so.

Today, the buffalo is merely another figure, though an important one, in the tapestry of remembrance. Someplace in the Forest of the Lost Children part of his great black body, now gone, has nourished the earth where he was born, lived, and died. Plants spring from it, birds and animals feed from it. As the buffalo has given new life to the forest, the unicorn—Nentikobe—has given man the opportunity to see the world in other terms. This book, more than proof of the existence of the unicorn in the natural world, is a defense of the right to exist of beauty and romantic imagination in that same world. Equally, it is a plea for conservation, for if man continues to destroy animals and their habitats at the present rate, then creatures as common to us as the lion and elephant will, in the future, be as rare and difficult to encounter as is today the unicorn.

The tapestries are changed with the whims of consciousness. Now reality is the smile on my face. The warm dogs in my arms. The bleached white buffalo skull at my feet. Reality is the truth that somewhere high on the Nguruman Escarpment, mane drifting in the wind, horn pointing south toward Ol Doinyo Lengai, the House of God, stands the Nentikobe. Reality is that to him, and there and then I must return.

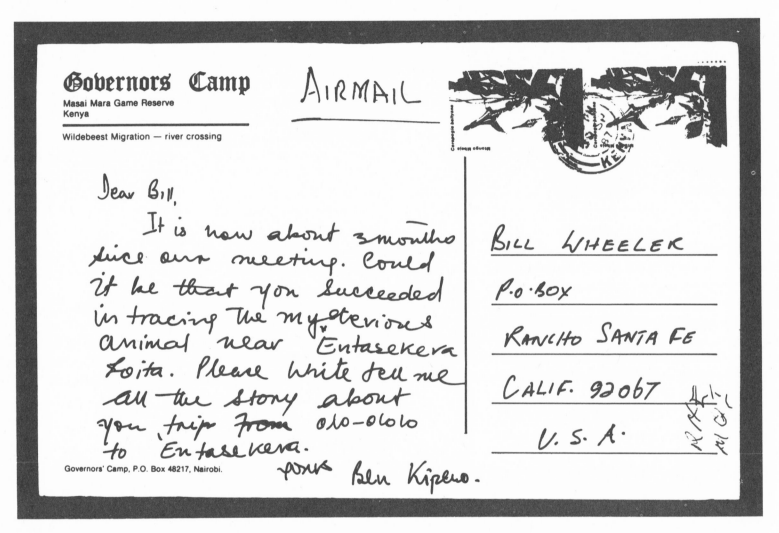

Governors Camp

Masai Mara Game Reserve
Kenya

Wildebeest Migration — river crossing

AIRMAIL

Dear Bill,

It is now about 3 months since our meeting. Could it be that you succeeded in tracing the mysterious animal near Entasekera Loita. Please write tell me all the story about your trip From olo-ololo to Entasekera.

yours   Ben Kipeno.

Governors' Camp, P.O. Box 48217, Nairobi.

BILL WHEELER

P.O. BOX

RANCHO SANTA FE

CALIF. 92067

U.S.A.

After returning to California, Bill Wheeler received this postcard from Ben Kipeno, the first Masai to have admitted to us the existence of the Nentikobe.

ACKNOWLEDGMENTS

Never will I be able to fully thank Dr. William Felix Wheeler for making the 1987 Elm Tree Unicorn Expedition possible. Not only did Bill provide the African experience and the Land Rover for our safari, but his presence also allowed us to share his sense of humor, his compassion and love for people, his hardheadedness, his sometimes foolhardy recklessness, his limitless generosity, and, most important of all, his friendship. He is one of the finest, most unique men that I have been privileged to know; and to him, for having made my childhood dreams of Africa reality, I will forever be indebted.

Joe Saccoman, my former assistant, not only photographed me in Africa, but also is, as is Bill Wheeler, responsible for many of the handsome images that make this book more complete. The success of the Elm Tree Expedition was in large part brought about because of Joe's enthusiasm, his sense of humor, his unfailing sense of friendship, his dedication, and his adventurous spirit.

Rick Fabares is a friend, talented artist, and photographic laboratory associate whose creative sensitivity and indefatigable devotion to this project will play a major part in any success that it may enjoy.

To Gene and Bonnie Brown I offer my deepest thanks for providing me with their exceedingly talented daughter, Lee Mitchelson, whose lovely, detailed drawings enrich these pages.

In Kenya, I am deeply grateful for their assistance and friendship to: Bill, Liz, and Doiky McGill, Simon Ole Makallah (warden of Masai Mara), Daniel Ole Mengoru and David, Shadrack Ole Lensir, Ben Kipeno, Vicky Chignell, Pat Beresford, Tim Ross, and to our Masai porters on the foot safari. For their assistance and compassion in those difficult hours and days following Joe's Cape buffalo injury, I thank Dr. Alberto Bencivenga, Elaine Leache, Robert Gichuki, and the staff of the Norfolk Hotel.

For preexpedition planning, deepest thanks go to close friends Gary and Lorian Stadler and to my trusty amigo David Kader; as well as to the Most Reverend and Mrs. Robert Q. Kennaugh, and Debra and T. R. Walter. For sharing their experience with animals on previous African trips, I thank Ron Whitfield, Rich Massena, Alan Roocroft, Jim Dolan, Larry Killmar, Ron Garrison, and Joan Embery and her husband, Duane Pillsbury.

To the many other persons who helped with preexpedition planning but are not listed here, I offer heartfelt thanks.

To Mike Scanlon and Award Prints of San Diego, gratitude is expressed for the care that they took with my work.

For their long hours typing this journal, I thank Judy Cotter, Gale Ebbson, and Julie Ebsen.

While designing this book, I counted on the expert advice of Barbara Chance and Scott Thom.

To my good friend José López, I express my gratitude for his interest in my work and for keeping my cameras functioning.

For their continued support of this project I thank (in Europe) Rudolf Blanckenstein and José Franco, and (in New York) my agent Gloria Loomis and at William Morrow, Larry Hughes, Al Marchioni, Sherry Arden, Lela Rolontz, Cheryl Asherman, Bernard Schleifer, and my new editor, Andy Ambraziejus. A good editor is almost as rare as is the unicorn, and it was my fortune to have Andy as friend and collaborator.

For the making of the color separations I thank Elias García, José Rosa and the staff at Teknocrom, as well as Cayfosa and Guillermo Matheu for doing such a fine job printing the book.

Ron and Gale Vavra, my brother and sister-in-law, and my mother I thank for taking care of me during the final editing of my journal.

To Rudolf O. Springer whatever thanks I offer are insufficient, for without his journal, my study could not even have been initiated.

To Africa, I express my love and gratitude for a debt that can never be repaid.

PHOTOGRAPHIC CREDITS

The majority of the photographs in this book were taken with Nikon cameras using Ektachrome and Kodachrome film. All Elm Tree Unicorn Expedition photographs were taken by the author with the exception of:

Wheeler—1, 6, 8, 11, 12, 22, 23, 24, 26, 28, 35, 40, 41, 44, 46, 47, 49, 50, 79, 84, 85, 87, 93, 94, 95, 98, 99, 121 (top), 128

Saccoman—13, 14, 15, 16, 17, 25, 29, 31, 32, 34, 38, 39, 61, 62, 65, 67, 68, 69, 70, 71, 72, 73, 74, 75, 76, 82, 83, 86, 89, 92, 96 (top), 102, 114, 115, 116

McGill—9, 10, 123, 124

McNamee—126, 127

Haddada ibis

PLANTS AND BUTTERFLIES

The butterflies and pressed plants that appear in this book were gathered in Kenya during the 1987 Elm Tree Unicorn Expedition. Each was encountered in an area where sightings of *Unicornuus africanus* were made.

216

CROM Princip gere · · · · S. Michl · · S. Naria

HISPANIA · · COR ·

MARE

OCEANVS ATLANTICVS

BA · RB · A ·

Golfo de las yeguas

Canarie insule · · · · ol: Fortunate · · · ·

TROPICVS CANCRI.

BL · LE · D ·

ARZANAGA · · · · GE · RIL

GVALATA · · · T: · · I · AE · DESER ·

NIGRITA · RVM ·

Insule Cap: Viridis olim Gorgades sine Hesperides

TONAVTO Niger

GAGO · · · GVBER

MELLI · · · DAVMA · · · · AENIN

MELEGETE

MAR · DEL · NORT.

RHINOCEROS · · · · · St THOME

HIPPOPOTAMVS

AEQVINOCTIALIS CIRCVLVS

RHINOCEROS

OCEANVS · · · · L · ETHIO

AFRICAM GRAECI LIBYCAPP.

BRESILIAE PARS.

AF · RI · CAE · TA · BVLA · NOVA.

II (

EDITA ANT · VERPIAE 1570

TROP ·